THE COMPLETE GUIDE TO FINANCIAL LITERACY FOR TEENS

BUILD REAL-WORLD MONEY MANAGEMENT SKILLS, AVOID LIVING PAYCHECK TO PAYCHECK, AND TAKE CHARGE OF YOUR FINANCIAL DESTINY

INCLUDES BUDGETING TOOLS!

HOLLY SHERMAN

CONTENTS

PART THREE

PART FOUR

PART FIVE

INTRODUCTION

Did you know that a single decision you make today could make you a millionaire in the future? That's the power of financial literacy, and it all starts here.

Financial literacy, or FinLit for short, is the understanding of financial concepts and skills, including investing, saving, budgeting, and borrowing, to name a few. If you want to be financially free, it's crucial that you are financially literate. And remember, you are never too young to start. The earlier you grasp these concepts and know how to apply them, the longer you will have to build on your financial freedom.

To help you along on your journey to being financially savvy, I want to introduce you to two teens who are also twins: David and Emma. Although they are the same age and have the same parents, their experience with money has been vastly different. They both grew up with little advice about money. Their parents haven't taught them how to work with money because they are financially uneducated themselves.

David, for instance, follows in his parents' footsteps. Whenever he receives his weekly allowance of $ 20, he spends it immediately on impulse buys like video games or snacks. Most of the time, he buys whatever catches his eye in the store. Little to no planning goes into his purchases, and he hasn't started a savings account because he doesn't feel like it's necessary at his age.

Emma, on the other hand, decided that she didn't want to live the same way her parents did. She wants to be financially free one day and have savings on hand when she needs it, without the need to take out a loan. She's money-savvy and plans all her purchases. Impulse buys are not part of her vocabulary, and she makes sure that every purchase is necessary and well thought through. Whenever she receives her paycheck or monetary gifts, she plans which portion she can spend and which portion needs to be saved.

As we work through the different chapters and concepts, we will revisit these twins to see how they deal with each topic.

If you are more like David than Emma at the moment, don't worry. You're not alone. According to a recent study by Stacey M. in 2024, only around 13% of teenagers in the U.S. have an understanding of finances. This is a concerning statistic, as financial literacy is a crucial life skill. Furthermore, around 75% of teenagers say that they learn about finances from their families (Jacimovic, 2023). If you do the math, that means that some teens are learning from their families but are not receiving enough information about the how-to.

When it comes to investing, around 48% of teens are turning to social media. While using social media is fun, 51.8% of teens would prefer money management to be taught in schools (Stacey M., 2024). Me too, teens, me too.

Although there may be hope for the future, it's not a big subject at the moment, so we need to find ways to fill the gaps. My parents tried their best to teach me growing up, but there were certain things I had to learn myself. I remember the first time I received an allowance. I had no idea what to do with it. I didn't know how to budget or save and found myself constantly waiting for next week's allowance - literally living from paycheck to paycheck, except I was a teenager, and I had no responsibilities. It was a frustrating time, but it also taught me the importance of financial literacy and the impact it can have on our lives.

One of the reasons it was so difficult was that it seemed like everyone else was always buying whatever was trending, and I wanted to fit in. Even at times when I managed to save a little money, if something came along that I wanted, I would spend it impulsively without thinking twice because there's just something about instant gratification. Even though I would regret the purchase later, the rush of delight I felt was enough to push me over the edge every time.

With all of this, I still had a hunger to learn more about money management - to actually be financially literate so that I could look forward to a secure future. Spending habits like what I just described won't lead to a financially free future unless you find a way to generate unlimited money.

Since most of us will never reach that level of income, we need to equip ourselves for the future. The younger you are when you start learning, the more you can apply the principles and cultivate healthy spending habits. If you're on the older side reading this book, don't worry! It's also never too late to start.

Through the years, I have learned and lost a lot. This book contains everything that you need to know to secure your financial future. Engage with it in a meaningful way, and you will:

- Understand the difference between needs and wants.
- Learn the value of money.
- Discover how to build credit.
- Learn how money can work for you.
- Discover different ways to invest.

Mastering these skills is the key to unlocking your financial freedom. And why is that important? Because financial freedom can open so many doors for you as a teen. By becoming financially free now, you will:

- Be able to cultivate healthy spending habits, which you will use well into your adult life.
- Be confident in your decision-making when it comes to money and living your life.
- Be able to pursue your hobbies, such as traveling, cosplay or sports.
- Live a happy life - since financial health is an essential pillar to a balanced life.
- Know how to make long-term investments to start accumulating interest now.
- Have the ability to plan for events and future endeavors, such as furthering your studies.

ROADMAP TO FINANCIAL MASTERY

We will follow a 6-phase roadmap to ensure that we cover all the necessary topics. The coming chapters will discuss these concepts in detail, providing you with a comprehensive understanding of each phase and how it contributes to your financial mastery.

Phase 1: Laying Your Financial Foundation

It's vital that we cover a few basic concepts to help lay the proper foundation before we get stuck in the details. These concepts will be discussed in Chapters 1 and 2.

Phase 2: Earning and Managing Income

For this phase, we will look at any income, including pocket money and paychecks, and also cover the deductions that you can expect. Chapters 3 and 4 are dedicated to this phase.

Phase 3: Banking and Financial Tools

Here, we will delve deeper into navigating the banking landscape in Chapter 5 and how to budget properly in Chapter 6.

Phase 4: Building Wealth and Financial Security

This is the only phase that consists of three chapters. We will look at saving (Chapter 7), investing (Chapter 8), and having a safety net (Chapter 9).

Phase 5: Credit, Debit, and Financial Responsibility

The overrated debate on whether credit cards are good or bad and how to be credit-wise is discussed in Chapter 10. After that, we look at big-ticket purchases (like buying a car) in Chapter 11.

Phase 6: Preparing for the Future and Giving Back

We will cover retirement (it's never too early to start) and giving back to the community in the last two chapters.

I don't know about you, but I'm ready to get this financial freedom train going. Grab something to take notes with, and make sure you understand the concepts in each chapter before moving on to the next.

Here we go!

PART ONE

CHAPTER 1
MASTERING MONEY: THE ART OF VALUE AND EXCHANGE

> *When money realizes that it is in good hands, it wants to stay and multiply in those hands.*

IDOWU KOYENIKAN,
INTERNATIONALLY RECOGNIZED
WEALTH CONSULTANT

What a thought-provoking quote! This is why those who have money always get more, and those who struggle do so until they learn how to manage their money properly. I don't know about you, but I definitely want to be part of the crowd who gets even more.

Before we get into it, it's important to discuss the basics of money. So, what is money?

UNDERSTANDING MONEY

Money is a tool we use in exchange for a product or service. For a second, let's imagine a world where money doesn't exist. How would you purchase goods? You will have to exchange something you have for something you want. The biggest problem with that is not all items have the same value. By introducing money, we can easily assign value to an item and make exchanges. Throughout history, shells, beads, salt, and precious metals have all served as money.

In his book Guide to Investing in Gold & Silver, Mike Maloney discusses the seven properties of money. Let's look at them briefly without boring you with too much detail.

- **Acceptability**: Money should be recognized and accepted by everyone in society as a tool for exchange.
- **Divisibility**: You should easily be able to divide money into smaller units without losing value.
- **Durability**: It should be durable, meaning that it must stand the test of time. Wear and tear should not affect it or decrease its value.
- **Fungibility**: You should be able to use money interchangeably with any other unit with the same value.
- **Limited supply**: It should be limited; otherwise, it loses its value. If money was easy to obtain, more people would have it, and it wouldn't be as valuable.
- **Portability**: It should be easy to transport or carry money.
- **Uniformity**: Money of the same value should all look the same.

MONEY VERSUS CURRENCY

Most people use the terms money and currency interchangeably, but they are different. To be considered money, an item must have all seven qualities you just read about. Examples of money include gold and silver coins and cryptocurrencies like Bitcoin.

But what about the U.S. dollar and money issued by other governments? At one time, most of these were money, too. Until 1973, the United States functioned on a "gold standard". That means every dollar in circulation could be redeemed for a **specific** amount of physical gold at any time.

But when the gold standard ended in 1972, U.S. dollars became currency – or more specifically, fiat currency – meaning it was backed only by the good faith of the federal government. One reason for changing the system was so the government could increase the money supply at their discretion. Since printing more dollars violates one of money's seven properties, they are no longer technically money. We'll look at the consequences of this decision a little later.

FORMS OF CURRENCY AND THEIR USES

Money performs many important functions in the economy, which is why it matters to everyone. One of the main functions is being a**n instrument** of **trade**. People all around the world accept currency **in exchange for** goods and services, making **commerce** easier and more efficient.

Ideally, currency would have the same value from country to country, i.e., $1 for €1. However, that is not the case. Each country has determined the value of its currency, and the exchange rate is influenced by many factors. At the time of this writing, 1 USD converts into 0.92 Euros.

Money is also a store of value or wealth. This means that money can be saved and used in the future, retaining its value over time. However, it's important to note that currency loses value over time due to inflation, a concept we will explore later.

Another function that might seem less evident is being a **means** of deferred payment. This is where credit cards and loans come in. They allow people to receive goods or services now and pay for them later, making it possible to manage finances more flexibly.

The value of any given currency is determined by supply and demand, which in turn is influenced by inflation, money supply, interest rates, and capital flow. For the scope of this book, we'll take a closer look at supply and demand, as well as inflation.

SUPPLY AND DEMAND

The concept of supply and demand is frequently mentioned in regard to the economy. It might seem complex, but it simply refers to the availability and desire for a particular product. "Supply" relates to the quantity of the item that is available, while "demand" indicates how much people want or need it.

Generally, if there is a high supply of an item, its value tends to be lower. Conversely, high demand for an item increases its value. Supply and demand usually have an inverse relationship: as demand increases, supply often decreases, making the item more valuable. Figure 1 explains the concept visually.

Consider a baseball card as an example. A common card with many copies in circulation isn't very valuable. However, a rare card with few copies available is highly prized and, therefore, more valuable because collectors are eager to obtain it.

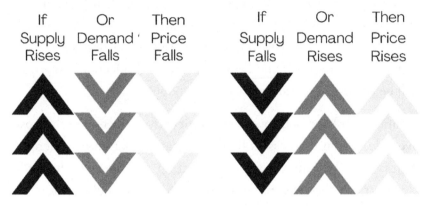

Figure 1 – Supply & Demand

Market equilibrium occurs when supply perfectly matches demand—there's just enough of the item to fulfill people's needs. This balance is dynamic, though, and can shift rapidly due to changes in supply or demand.

Inflation

Inflation is essentially the increase in prices over time, which reduces the purchasing power of money. This means that the same amount of money buys less than it did in the past. For instance, $100 today doesn't go as far as it did ten years ago.

As inflation rises, the value of money declines, meaning you can buy less with the same amount of cash. To illustrate, consider the cost of a cup of coffee. In 2000, a cup cost about $1.00. Fast forward to today, and a tall Americano at Starbucks is priced at

$3.25, marking a 325% price increase over 24 years. While this change occurred over two decades, it's important to recognize that inflation causes the price of all products to rise, not just coffee.

Inflation is unavoidable, but there are strategies to mitigate its impact on our finances. Being financially literate (FinLit) helps us make wise decisions, such as where to invest to outpace inflation, owning assets like gold, maintaining high-interest savings accounts, managing debt wisely, and keeping a careful budget. These topics will be covered in detail in upcoming chapters.

Inflation can have both positive and negative effects. On the positive side, if you own assets like real estate, inflation can increase their value, potentially allowing you to sell at a profit later. However, on the negative side, inflation means higher prices for buyers and an overall increase in the cost of living. If wages don't keep pace with inflation, maintaining a particular lifestyle becomes more challenging.

Some of the factors that influence inflation include the following:

Money supply expansion: This is the primary cause of inflation. As soon as the supply of currency increases, inflation increases. An increase in currency supply is driven by the rise in printing and distributing more money and legally decreasing the value of the country's currency.

Exchange rates: As discussed earlier, the exchange rate is the value of one currency relative to another. When the value of a currency increases, the exchange rate will increase, which will result in a decrease in the price of imported goods. In simpler terms, the higher the exchange rate, the cheaper it will be to import goods from other countries where the value of the currency is lower.

Government regulation: It's the government's job to control inflation and ensure that it doesn't become unmanageable. They use specific rules and tools to monitor and manage inflation.

Growing economy: A growing economy is good news; however, if the economy grows too quickly, this could lead to inflation. A growing economy means there are more people and more businesses, which means that demand for specific products or services will increase.

CRYPTOCURRENCY

We won't go into too much detail here because its outside the scope of this book, but it's essential to understand the basics.

Cryptocurrency is a digital form of money that doesn't rely on banks to verify transactions. It's a peer-to-peer system that lets anyone anywhere send and receive payments. Instead of being printed like dollars or euros, cryptocurrencies are produced by computers all over the world using free software. Every transaction is recorded in a public list called the blockchain, which helps ensure that everything is transparent and checks are in place to keep it secure.

Bitcoin, created in 2009, is the most well-known cryptocurrency. Even though it sounds like it's been around for a while, it's not used as commonly as regular currency. Most people buy and hold cryptocurrencies like they would stocks, hoping to sell them for more than they paid as their prices go up.

Being financially free and having a steady supply of money has a myriad of benefits, including the following:

- **Pursuing your passion and dreams**: Having money means that you can pursue your passion and fulfill your dreams—buy the home you want, go on that extravagant vacation, start your own business, etc.
- **Freedom**: Having enough money gives you freedom. You can choose where and how you want to live, pursue your hobbies, make sure your needs are met, and have a security fund for emergencies.
- **Provides security and reduces financial stress**: Money offers a level of security so that you don't have to worry about having a roof over your head, where the next meal will come from, or even covering healthcare expenses. It gives you the peace of mind to know your needs are taken care of.
- **Opens the door for more life experiences:** Although many activities in life are free, sometimes you need money to experience them to their fullest. Think family vacations, pro sporting events, fancy restaurants, and any other activity that offers an over-the-top experience.

Regardless of how much money you have, it may feel like you need more. The secret is reaching a point where you feel like you have it under control. Money should never control you or what you think you can or can't do. It is a tool we use and should be managed as such.

NEXT STEPS AND CHAPTER QUESTIONS

At the end of each chapter, I have included activities and questions to put you on the *FinLit Fast Track* and help you put your new knowledge into practice. There is also a checklist at the end of the book to track your progress. Before moving ahead, reflect on what you've learned and make sure that you have a good understanding of the concepts. While working through these activities and questions, don't hesitate to go back to the section in the chapter if you need to reread the information.

FinLit Fast Track

Activities

1. Start a conversation about money with your family or friends. Share what you've learned or ask them to help you understand concepts that are still unclear.
2. Learn more about the differences between money and currency by watching Mike Maloney's video series "The Hidden Secrets of Money." It's available here: https://FinLitFastTrack.com/hidden-secrets/.
3. See how much your favorite beverage will cost in the future by using the inflation calculator at https://FinLitFastTrack.com/inflation-calc.

Questions

When working through these questions, you might find it helpful to write down your answers in a dedicated notebook and discuss them with someone else.

1. Can you explain the differences between money and currency in your own words?
2. How does inflation impact your purchasing power and financial choices? Have you noticed its effects in your lifetime? How does it make you feel?

3. What intrigues you the most about cryptocurrencies?
4. Reflect on a time when you observed the principles of supply and demand affecting the value of a product you wanted. Did it affect your decision to buy it?

You've taken the first step toward building your financial knowledge, and I hope you now have a clearer understanding of the monetary forces at play in your life. The next chapter explores the concept of the money mindset. Understanding your money mindset is the key to unlocking a world of financial possibilities, and we're excited to guide you on this enlightening journey. Let's dive in!

CHAPTER 2
HARNESSING YOUR MONEY MINDSET FOR THE FUTURE

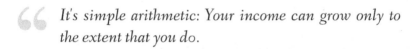

It's simple arithmetic: Your income can grow only to the extent that you do.

T. HARV EKER, AUTHOR, BUSINESSMAN AND MOTIVATIONAL SPEAKER

Have you ever stopped to think how your mindset can affect every aspect of your life? We often accept that it is what it is. But truthfully, our mindset plays a more significant role than we sometimes realize. Our brains are pretty powerful and can either help us succeed or make us feel inadequate or undeserving.

How we see and understand money influences how we spend it. If we go back to the twins from the introduction, David and Emma, it's clear that David's mindset needs some work. His idea of what money is and what it can do for him is vastly different from Emma's. As a result, Emma is in a much better financial position than David, even though they grew up the same way and had access to the same resources.

Exploring whether money can buy happiness is a classic debate. The answer isn't straightforward—it really depends on what happiness means to you. For some people, happiness isn't tied to the amount of money they have. They might not be wealthy, but they're content and happy with their lives. On the other hand, some people can afford anything they want but still feel something is missing.

Imagine someone who's been struggling to make ends meet. For them, just having enough money to cover basic needs like food, shelter, and clothing can bring a huge relief and boost their happiness. That's because the stress of not being able to meet these needs can make anyone feel unhappy.

However, for someone who has always had enough, happiness might be linked to other, harder-to-achieve goals. In such cases, simply having more money doesn't guarantee happiness. This shows that the impact of money on our happiness changes based on our personal experiences and what we're used to.

Additionally, how we handle money plays a significant role. Someone might feel a rush of happiness from buying something on impulse, but this short-term joy can lead to long-term stress if it puts them in financial trouble. Ultimately, our money habits reflect our beliefs and attitudes about money. How we choose to spend can either contribute to our happiness or detract from it, highlighting the importance of a mindful approach to money.

Talking about money can be challenging. In many families, it's a subject that people avoid, and not sticking to a budget is common. These habits stem from particular unhealthy views about money. Maybe you've noticed some of these attitudes in your own life:

- Feeling guilty whenever you spend money.
- Not setting or following through on financial goals.
- Believing that spending money is the only way to have fun.
- Carrying high credit card debt.
- Often worrying about not having enough money.

If any of these sound familiar, don't stress! You can develop a healthier outlook on money. Improving your financial mindset starts with changing how you view and handle your finances.

Developing financial confidence is a journey of personal growth and empowerment. It's about equipping yourself with the knowledge and skills to manage your money effectively. It's about building a positive relationship with money, where you feel in control and optimistic about your financial future. This confidence doesn't appear overnight; it grows as you gain more experience and learn to manage your money wisely. Remember, everyone starts somewhere, and there's always an opportunity to enhance your financial skills and confidence.

Before we dive deep into this chapter, let's talk about some ways you can start boosting your financial confidence right now:

- **Take Action Now**: Don't wait for the perfect moment to take control of your financial life. One of the most empowering steps you can take is to start making changes today. For instance, if your goal is to buy a house by the time you're 25, begin by researching what's needed for a home loan. You don't need to have all the answers to start making progress. Remember, every small step counts towards your financial success.

- **Plan for the future**: Knowing what you're working towards can make a big difference. Setting financial goals helps guide your decisions and boosts your confidence as you see yourself making progress.

- **Increase your financial knowledge**: Becoming more financially literate can make you feel more confident about your money decisions. The more you know, the more empowered you'll be to apply that knowledge effectively.

- **Learn to budget**: We'll cover this more in later chapters, but understanding how to manage a budget is crucial. It gives you a clear picture of where your money goes and how much you have to spend, which can really boost your confidence.

- **Start investing:** Don't wait for the "perfect" time to invest because there's no such thing. The best time to start is now. Even a little research and small investments can begin to grow your wealth.

- **Pay off debt:** If you have debt, plan to pay it off quickly. Debt can weigh you down and make you feel like you'll never be financially free.

- **Examine your money mindset:** We'll explore the concept of a money mindset next and how you can develop a healthy one that supports your financial goals.

By addressing these areas, you can start to feel more in control of your financial future and more confident in your ability to manage money.

MONEY BELIEFS

Our beliefs about money shape our money mindset. This includes our thoughts on what we can do with money, where it comes from, how to manage it, and its importance in our lives. This mindset influences how we spend and save money and even how we talk about it. Essentially, you can have a positive or negative view of money.

A negative money mindset often involves procrastination, feeling overwhelmed or intimidated by financial decisions, and viewing money management as a daunting task. On the other hand, a positive money mindset makes it easier to make financial decisions, see opportunities instead of obstacles, set and achieve financial goals, seek help when needed, and understand that financial situations can be improved.

It's important to note that developing a healthy money mindset isn't about blame. Our money mindsets begin forming at a very young age, influenced by how the people around us handle money and the financial behaviors we observe. Even well-meaning comments from parents like "Money doesn't grow on trees" or "You have to work hard for your money" can unintentionally foster a negative view of money. But the good news is, these mindsets can be changed with awareness and effort, and you have the power to do so.

Changing a negative money mindset into a positive one is possible. It starts by recognizing those ingrained beliefs and understanding that every financial situation has a solution. Awareness and education are key to transforming how you view and interact with money. This shift not only improves your financial well-being but can also lead to a more fulfilled and less stressful life.

Understanding your beliefs about money is crucial in improving your financial relationship. Many of us hold onto limiting beliefs that can block our path to financial success. It's important to recognize these beliefs and work to replace them with healthier, more positive attitudes about money. Here are some common limiting beliefs—see if any of these sound familiar to you:

- "I'll never make as much money as my friends."
- "We've never been rich; it's just not who we are."
- "Rich people are bad people."
- "People who are rich are rude."
- "I'm not good enough to make more money."
- "I'm not educated enough to earn more."
- "To make money, you need money."

If you find yourself nodding to any of these, it's a sign to start shifting how you think about money. Challenging these beliefs can open up new possibilities and ways to approach your finances that you might not have considered before.

Even if you feel you already have a positive money mindset, don't skip over this part. There's always room to grow and improve. Each section in this book is designed to help you enhance your understanding and management of money, and you might discover some valuable insights that can take your financial thinking to the next level.

If, like David, you're looking to shift from a negative to a more abundant money mindset, here are some practical steps you can take:

- **Believe in Your Success**: The first step is to believe that you are capable and deserving of success. It doesn't matter your background, whether rich or poor—success is attainable for anyone.

- **Commit to Your Success:** Once you believe in your ability to succeed, commit to it. Promise yourself that no matter what challenges come your way, you will achieve success. This commitment will help build your resilience and keep you focused on your goals.

- **Read Inspirational Books:** Reading can significantly influence your mindset. Look for books that positively impact your outlook, not just about money but about self-confidence and personal growth. Self-help, motivational, and leadership books can all contribute to a stronger, more positive mindset.

- **Stay in Control:** Remember, you control your money; it doesn't control you. Money is a tool to manage your life. Keep reminding yourself that you make the decisions about how you earn, save, and spend your money.

- **Embrace Generosity:** Adopting a mindset of generosity can profoundly affect how you view money. Holding onto money too tightly can be fear-based, but letting go and using it to help others can redefine its role in your life. It's not about giving away everything you have, but perhaps doing small things, like paying for someone's coffee or donating to a cause you care about. Acts of generosity can enrich your sense of well-being and dramatically shift your attitude toward money.

By following these steps, you can start to cultivate a healthier relationship with money, one that sees it as a positive force in your life and the lives of others.

MONEY PERSONALITIES

An important yet often overlooked aspect of financial literacy is the concept of money personalities. Understanding that financial behaviors are not "one-size-fits-all" is crucial; we all have unique money personalities that influence our financial decisions and mindset. Just as understanding someone's love language can enhance your relationship with them, knowing your money personality can help you identify your spending and saving habits and make necessary adjustments.

According to financial experts, there are five main money personality types:

The Gambler: Gamblers are willing to take significant risks with their money for the potential of a high return. This desire for a big payoff can sometimes lead to risky behaviors, such as selling possessions to invest more in high-stake opportunities, which can lead to financial ruin if not carefully managed.

The Giver: Givers enjoy using their resources to support others, often donating to causes and helping those around them. While their generosity is commendable, it can sometimes lead to financial strain or debt if they don't balance their altruism with their own financial needs.

The Saver: Savers are the opposite of spenders; they prefer to save money and are often seen as frugal. While saving is generally positive, excessive saving can lead to missed experiences and a lack of enjoyment in life, as savers may hesitate to spend on hobbies or new experiences.

The Spender: Spenders enjoy buying things, whether for themselves or others and are drawn to the instant gratification that spending provides. However, this can become problematic if spending leads to debt, especially if they spend more money than they have, potentially leading to financial difficulties such as bankruptcy.

The Worrier: Worriers are constantly anxious about their finances, regardless of how much money they actually have. This continual worry can detract from their quality of life, as it can prevent them from enjoying the present and lead to significant stress and anxiety.

Recognizing which of these profiles best describes you can be the first step in refining your financial habits to foster a healthier relationship with money.

INSTANT GRATIFICATION

We live in a world where instant gratification has become the norm. Instant gratification is the immediate satisfaction we get from indulging in what we want right away. For example, imagine walking into a store, seeing a shirt you love, and buying it on the spot. The happiness you feel from making that immediate purchase is a classic example of instant gratification. On the other hand, delayed gratification involves waiting to buy something until you can comfortably afford it. While the bliss might be delayed, it is just as satisfying, if not more, because it comes without financial stress.

The allure of instant gratification often stems from our desire to experience happiness immediately. We think, "If I have the money now, why not spend it?" This mindset can overlook the needs of our future selves—who might need that money for other essential expenses later in the month.

Falling into the habit of impulsive spending can significantly impact our finances. Consider our twins, David and Emma. David tends to buy whatever he wants right away, often making unnecessary purchases that deplete his funds quickly. Emma, in contrast, plans and saves for her purchases. She only buys items that bring value to her life. As a result, she manages to save consistently and has money available for important expenses when they arise.

To achieve financial freedom, it's crucial to cultivate more self-control and shift towards delayed gratification. Here are a few practical steps to help develop this habit:

- **Set Clear Financial Goals:** Knowing what you're saving for can help you avoid unnecessary purchases.
- **Wait Before You Buy:** When you see something you want, wait a few days before you buy it. This can help you determine if it's a genuine need or just a fleeting want. When I'm out shopping and see something I think I want, I walk around the store with it for a while, maybe half an hour or so, and nine times out of 10, I change my mind about buying it. Try it sometime. It really works.
- **Budget for Fun:** Allocate a specific amount of your budget for discretionary spending. This allows you to enjoy some immediate purchases without compromising your financial goals.
- **Visualize the Benefits:** Regularly remind yourself of the benefits of saving and how delayed gratification will help you achieve your long-term financial objectives. Creating a vision board that includes pictures of your goals can be just the inspiration you need to stick to your goals.

- **Avoid Temptation:** It's essential to recognize where you're most vulnerable to impulse buys and steer clear of these temptations. If you find it hard to resist a sale, avoid the sales sections in stores or websites known for constant discounts. If online shopping triggers spontaneous purchases, consider limiting your time on these websites. The best way to manage temptation is by not facing it in the first place.
- **Seek Accountability:** Having someone who can help keep your spending in check can be invaluable. Choose a trusted friend or family member you can contact whenever you're tempted to make an impulse purchase. Explain to them that you're trying to save and discuss why you want to make a particular purchase. Often, just talking about it can help you think twice and decide against buying on impulse. This practice reinforces your goals and strengthens your resolve to practice delayed gratification.

FinLit Fast Track

Activities

1. If you haven't done so already, determine your money personality. What aspects of your personality would you consider positive? Which ones may you want to change or improve on?
2. To help alter your money mindset, here are some money mantras to recite:

- My attitude toward money is positive and I have the ability to spend it wisely.
- I deserve to be financially stable and prosperous.
- I am in control of my finances and financial wellness.
- Money can't control me, I control money.
- I deserve to be successful.
- Money is a tool I use to achieve my goals.
- I am on my way to leading a successful and wealthy life.
- Saving money is good for my future self.
- I only spend my money on things I value.
- I am financially confident.
- I deserve to live a fulfilling life, and smart financial decisions can support that.
- I use money to open new opportunities.
- I am improving my relationship with money every day.

Questions

1. What is the most important thing you learned in this chapter?
2. What are some of the beliefs your parents or other adults you know have about money? What kind of lifestyle do they have?
3. How do you think a poor money mindset would impact other areas of your life?

Recognizing the importance of cultivating a positive money mindset and preparing for your financial future through wise investments is a significant step toward achieving financial success.

In part II, we will focus on income and income taxes. In the next chapter, we will shift our focus to the practical side of financial literacy—earning money. We'll delve into strategies for earning income, whether through part-time jobs or entrepreneurial ventures. We're here to guide you on this exciting journey. Let's get started!

PART TWO

PART TWO

CHAPTER 3
FROM POCKET MONEY TO PAYCHECKS

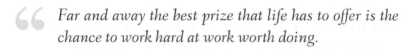 *Far and away the best prize that life has to offer is the chance to work hard at work worth doing.*

THEODORE ROOSEVELT, 26TH PRESIDENT OF THE UNITED STATES

Have you ever given this much thought? I'll be honest—I used to wing it and hope for the best. But if there is one piece of advice that you should take to heart, it's this quote.

Perhaps you're in a situation similar to mine. Back when I was a teenager, I was just getting an allowance and yearning for more financial freedom. I was eager to earn my own paycheck, envisioning the thrill of buying whatever I wanted, whenever I wanted. But when I started exploring job opportunities, I was hit with a wave of uncertainty. I wasn't sure what I'd enjoy doing, what to look out for, or if my job choices at that age even mattered.

In this chapter, we want to help you understand the various strategies and opportunities for earning money as a teen. This knowledge will not only help you build a solid financial foundation but also guide you toward future stability and success. Let's start by exploring why it's beneficial to get a job during your teenage years instead of waiting until you're an adult.

Here are several compelling reasons to start working young:

- **Earn Your Own Income**: When you earn your own income, you gain the power to buy the things you want or need without relying on your parents. Whether it's brand-name clothes, the latest smartphone, or a trip to an amusement park, you can make these purchases on your own.
- **Value Money More:** It's easy to take things for granted when you get them for free. When you start earning and spending your own money, you'll likely appreciate it more because you understand the effort it took to earn it. This might even make you think twice before splurging on unnecessary items.
- **Explore Different Jobs:** Your teenage years are a time of discovery. Not everyone knows what they want to do for a career at a young age. Working in your teenage years lets you try out different fields, opening doors to new experiences and possibilities. This can prevent you from ending up in a job you dislike later on.
- **Develop Work Ethics and Skills**: Starting work in your teens can teach you valuable work ethics and skills that will benefit you throughout your life. Jobs teach you how to interact with different personalities, meet targets,

and manage conflicts. These are skills your peers may not have if they haven't worked yet.

- **Learn Money Management:** One of the biggest benefits of working as a teen is the sense of accomplishment that comes with learning how to handle money firsthand. You'll learn about budgeting, saving, and the true cost of items, which is invaluable knowledge for your future. This early financial education can help you make smarter decisions and set you up for a more secure future.

Getting a job as a teen is more than just about making money—it's about setting the groundwork for your future in many ways, from understanding the value of hard work to managing finances effectively.

THE BASICS OF EMPLOYMENT

Transitioning from receiving an allowance to earning an income is a significant step. It's normal to feel nervous about starting your first job, especially when you're unsure about what to expect.

Here are some essential tips to help you excel in your new role and make a great impression:

- **Punctuality Matters:** Being on time is a simple yet crucial aspect of professionalism. Being late can negatively impact your performance and give the impression that you lack a strong work ethic. Arriving at work early helps you feel more prepared and calmer.
- **Be Open to Advice**: Experienced colleagues can provide invaluable guidance. Listen attentively when

they offer advice. If something doesn't seem right, double-check with your employer, but respect the wisdom of experience.

- **Understand Workplace Boundaries:** When new to a job, it's wise to avoid asking for significant favors like extended vacations or long lunches. Prove your reliability first. Demonstrating your dedication and reliability can lead to more flexibility later on.

- **Maintain a Professional Image:** Your appearance makes an impression. Dress neatly and practice good hygiene. You don't need expensive clothes or makeup—just ensure you look clean and put-together.

- **Build Relationships:** Forming connections with colleagues can make your workdays more enjoyable and provide a support network. Don't hesitate to reach out and make friends, even if they are older than you.

- **Clarify Your Responsibilities:** On your first day, make sure you understand what is expected of you. Ask for a clear list of responsibilities to ensure you meet your employer's expectations.

- **Balance Your Life:** It's important to balance work with your studies and social life. Managing your time effectively from a young age is a skill that will benefit you indefinitely. Here's how you can maintain this balance:

  - **Use a Time Budget:** Plan your day just like you would with a financial budget. Allocate specific times for work, study, and leisure, and stick to this schedule as much as possible.
  - **Make Work Fun:** Find ways to incorporate social elements into your job. This can make it easier to merge work with your social life.

○ **Combat Procrastination:** Procrastination can waste a surprising amount of time. Look for strategies to overcome this habit, such as breaking tasks into smaller, manageable steps or setting deadlines for yourself.

By following these guidelines, you'll not only perform well in your job but also lay a strong foundation for your career and personal development.

EMPLOYEE VS. INDEPENDENT CONTRACTOR

As you delve into job options, you'll likely come across two main paths: becoming an employee (whether temporary or permanent) or working as an independent contractor. Each option has its own set of benefits and challenges, and the right choice for you will depend on how you like to work. This guide also explores the intriguing concept of being a "teenpreneur," which is more akin to being an independent contractor.

To help you understand the differences, let's simplify it: If you work at an office or another facility where the company provides everything you need for your job, you're considered an employee. However, suppose you're someone like a freelance photographer or makeup artist who uses their own equipment and supplies for work. In that case, you're operating as an independent contractor.

Choosing between being an employee or an independent contractor involves weighing various pros and cons based on your personal circumstances, career goals, and preferences. Here's a breakdown of the advantages and disadvantages of each option:

BEING AN EMPLOYEE

+ *Pros:*

- **Stability**: Employees usually receive a steady paycheck and can rely on a regular income. This financial stability is crucial for long-term planning and securing loans or mortgages.
- **Benefits**: Many employers offer benefits such as health insurance, retirement plans, paid vacation, and sick leave. These benefits can significantly enhance your overall compensation package and financial security.
- **Less Administrative Work:** As an employee, you don't have to worry about the paperwork and taxes associated with running a business. The employer handles payroll deductions like taxes and social security contributions.
- **Career Advancement:** Being part of an organization provides opportunities for training and career progression. Based on performance and tenure, you can climb up the corporate ladder.

− *Cons:*

- **Limited Control:** Employees have less control over their work hours, tasks, and, sometimes, their work environment. They must adhere to the company's policies and directives.
- **Dependence on Employer:** Your employment security is tied to the company's fortunes and managerial

decisions, which can lead to job loss if the business downsizes or shuts down.

- **Less Tax Flexibility:** Employees can't deduct work-related expenses in the same way independent contractors can, which may lead to higher taxable income.

BEING AN INDEPENDENT CONTRACTOR

+ *Pros:*

- **Flexibility**: Independent contractors can often set their own schedules and choose the projects they want to work on, providing a great deal of flexibility and autonomy.
- **Higher Earning Potential:** Contractors can potentially earn more, especially if they manage multiple clients or specialize in high-demand skills. They can adjust their rates according to the market and their expertise.
- **Tax Benefits**: Independent contractors can deduct business expenses from their taxes, which can include home office costs, equipment, travel, and more, potentially lowering their taxable income.
- **Choice of Work:** Contractors have the freedom to pick their clients and projects, which can lead to greater job satisfaction if they choose projects aligned with their interests.

— *Cons:*

- **Financial Instability:** Income can be irregular and unpredictable, making financial planning more challenging. Contractors must often save during lucrative periods to cover times when work is scarce.
- **No Employer Benefits:** Independent contractors are not eligible for benefits like health insurance or retirement plans through their clients and must arrange and fund these themselves.
- **Administrative Overhead:** Contractors must manage their own invoicing, contracts, taxes, and other administrative tasks, which can be time-consuming.
- **Less Job Security:** Work can be more sporadic and dependent on continually finding new clients and projects, leading to less job security than traditional employment.

Each path offers distinct opportunities and challenges, and the best choice depends on your personal preferences, financial needs, career goals, and tolerance for risk.

So, how do you decide whether to be an employee or an independent contractor? There's no right or wrong choice; it really depends on what suits you best. Some people flourish with the freedom of being an independent contractor. In contrast, others prefer the stability and structure that come with being an employee. Consider what makes you happiest and where you think you'll thrive. Both options come with their own stresses, so think about which challenges you're better equipped to handle. Review the pros and cons listed above and decide which set of drawbacks you're most comfortable dealing with. This will help guide you toward the choice that best aligns with your personal and professional goals.

BECOMING A TEENPRENEUR

Starting your own business and being the boss sounds exciting. Still, there's a lot to think about before you can truly call yourself a teenpreneur—a teen entrepreneur. Here are some benefits of starting your own business while you're still a teen:

- **Financial Skills:** Running your own business is a crash course in money management. There's no better way to learn how to handle finances than by managing your business's budget.
- **Creativity**: Owning a business allows you to channel your creativity into something productive. Pursuing your passion can make you happier and more fulfilled.
- **Time Management:** As a business owner, you'll quickly learn how to manage your time effectively. Knowing what needs to be done and by when is crucial for business success.
- **Resilience**: Some things will go differently than planned, and running a business will teach you how to adapt and solve problems quickly. This builds incredible resilience.

If these challenges excite you, entrepreneurship might be your path. Remember, being an entrepreneur can be stressful since you depend on yourself and your clients for income. However, you can start small—many successful businesses began as side hustles.

Now, let's walk through the steps to launching a business as a teenpreneur:

1. Idea and Research: Identify what type of business you want to start. Conduct market research to ensure there's a demand for your product or service. For example, if you're considering tutoring, check if there's enough demand in your area that is not already covered by others.

2. Business Registration: Depending on your business scope, you might need to register it:

- Sole Proprietorship: Ideal for small, low-risk businesses.
- Partnership: If you're starting a business with others.
- LLC (Limited Liability Company): Offers protection for your personal assets against business liabilities.
- C Corporation and S Corporation: More complex structures suited for larger businesses. You probably won't need this as a teen.

3. Business Operations: Decide on your business location, what services or products you'll offer, whether you need employees, what equipment you'll need, how you'll handle finances, and your marketing strategy.

4. Regulations and Taxes: While we won't cover this in detail here, make sure to research any necessary licenses, tax obligations, and legal requirements for starting and running a business as a teen.

5. Learn from Others: Talk to other entrepreneurs or research online to learn from their experiences and challenges. This can help you avoid common pitfalls and accelerate your success.

By understanding these steps and preparing accordingly, you can set a strong foundation for your business and gain valuable skills that will benefit you throughout your life.

Opening your own coffee shop as a teenager might be unrealistic, but there are so many other businesses you can start as a teen. One of the most fulfilling ways to earn a living is by turning your skills and hobbies into a career. This approach ensures that you not only enjoy your job but also get to engage in your passions while earning money. Start by writing down all the skills you excel at and the hobbies you love. Next, figure out which of these can generate income. From there, you can begin exploring how to transform your interests into a profitable venture.

Here are some ideas to get your creative juices flowing:

- Babysitting
- Tutoring
- Detailing cars
- Selling arts and crafts
- Dog walking
- House and pet sitting
- Giving music lessons
- Selling baked goods
- Mowing lawns / shoveling snow

FinLit Fast Track

Activities

1. If you're ready to get a job:

- Choose several places you might like to work and ask an employee at each place how s/he likes it there.
- Create a weekly calendar and block off all your current obligations like school, athletic practice and church. How many hours are left for you to work?
- If you don't have your own car, discuss with your parents how you would get to your job.

2. If you think you'd like to start a business:

- *Side Hustle Nation* is a great place to research business ideas that are suitable for teens. Check them out here: https://FinLitFastTrack.com/teen-side-hustles.
- After exploring the site, use the business brainstorming questionnaire below to help you narrow down your options.
- Check with your local chamber of commerce to see if there is a young entrepreneur program you can join. Besides walking you through starting a business, they pair you with a local business owner who acts as your mentor for the duration of the program.

Business Idea Brainstorm Questionnaire

- What am I good at or passionate about?
- What product or service can I provide that aligns with my skills and passions?
- Are any of these products and services on my list missing from my community?
- Who is most likely to buy my product or service?
- What other businesses in my area already offer this product or service?
- In what way can I make my product or service stand out from theirs?

Questions

1. What is my reason for starting my own business?
2. How does starting this business help me achieve my goals?
3. What research do I need to do to ensure I have all the knowledge required to run this business?
4. Is this something I will enjoy doing for years to come or am I looking for something for the short-term?
5. What does my support system look like? This can be family and friends, or anyone who is on board and willing to support you.

We explored various strategies for generating income, from part-time jobs to entrepreneurial ventures, and the importance of building a strong financial foundation.

In the next chapter, we will dive into the world of income taxes. You'll gain a comprehensive understanding of how taxes work, your responsibilities as a taxpayer, and strategies for optimizing your tax situation.

CHAPTER 4
FROM EARNINGS TO DEDUCTIONS

 Nothing is certain but death and taxes.

BENJAMIN FRANKLIN, FOUNDING FATHER OF THE UNITED STATES

Like it or not, taxes are a part of life. We pay taxes on almost everything, and the sooner we accept their permanence, the more at peace we can be about handling them. In this book, we're going to zero in on income taxes, though it's good to remember there are many types of taxes out there.

If you've ever had a job and received a paycheck, you might have noticed deductions for income tax on your pay stub. If you haven't seen this yet, don't worry—we'll go over a typical pay stub together.

UNDERSTANDING A PAY STUB

When you're employed, you receive a pay stub with your paycheck, regardless of whether your wages are deposited directly into your bank account. This stub can be either a physical document or an electronic one and details the calculations made from your gross pay to determine your net income, including any additions or deductions.

A pay stub typically includes the following elements:

- Pay Period: It shows the period for which the payment is made, your hourly rate, and the total hours worked.
- Employer and Employee Information: This includes the names, addresses, and contact details of both the employer and the employee.
- Employee Benefit Deductions: Some benefits, like health insurance, may be partially paid by deducting amounts from your gross pay.
- Gross Pay: This is calculated by multiplying your hourly pay rate by the total number of hours worked.
- Voluntary Deductions: These are amounts you might choose to have withheld for personal reasons, such as donations to charities.
- Tax Deductions: The pay stub should list all taxes withheld by the employer, including federal, state, Social Security (SS FICA), and Medicare (FICA MED) taxes.
- Net Pay: This is your take-home pay after all deductions are accounted for.
- Year-to-Date Totals (YTD): These figures show your cumulative gross and net earnings and total deductions for the year.

| Business Name | | | | | EARNINGS STATEMENT | |
| Business Address | | | | | | |

EMPLOYEE NAME			SSN	EMPLOYEE ID	CHECK NO.	PAY PERIOD	PAY DATE
Terri Teenager					91433	05/23/2024 - 06/05/2024	06/09/2024

INCOME	RATE	HOURS	CURRENT TOTAL	DEDUCTIONS	CURRENT TOTAL	YEAR-TO-DATE
GROSS WAGES	12.00	23.00	276.00	FICA MED TAX	4.00	48.02
				FICA SS TAX	17.11	205.34
				FED TAX	0.00	0.00
				IL ST TAX	8.38	100.56

YTD GROSS	YTD DEDUCTIONS	YTD NET PAY	CURRENT TOTAL	CURRENT DEDUCTIONS	NET PAY
3,312.00	353.93	2,958.07	276.00	29.49	246.51

Figure 2 - Sample Pay Stub Courtesy of Pay-Stub.com

Receiving your first pay stub is an exciting moment, and soon enough, you'll be getting one regularly—whether that's weekly, bi-weekly, or monthly. Make sure you always review it for accuracy and tell your manager immediately if you find an error. As these accumulate, you might wonder what to do with the older ones. Hold onto them—financial experts recommend keeping each pay stub for at least a year. Consider making digital copies to preserve them even longer. This way, you'll have them handy for referencing during tax time or resolving any discrepancies that might arise.

TAXES 101

As seen above, quite a few taxes can be deducted from your paycheck. Everyone must pay federal income tax, but only 42 states and Washington D.C. have a state income tax. Additionally, a few of the larger cities, such as St. Louis and Philadelphia, also collect a city income tax.

You might be wondering if all income is taxable, and the answer is most of it. Here's a list of the types that are:

- wages from a job
- sales made by your business
- self-employment income (including side hustles)
- dividends, interest, and capital gains from investments
- benefits you receive, such as unemployment income

Most people will only file one state income tax return if they live and work in the same state. However, if you live and work in different states, you will need to file more than one return. The deadline to file state and federal income tax returns is April 15th every year.

SOCIAL SECURITY TAXES

Social Security taxes are collected to provide income and health-care to those who have retired or are disabled. You may have heard your grandparents or other older adults talk about their Social Security checks and Medicare benefits. These taxes are deducted from the paychecks of working people and paid to those who have reached retirement age, which is 67 at this time. There is a limit to how much can be deducted from your paycheck; however, most people's incomes don't reach this threshold.

Tax Brackets

For 2024, tax brackets and rates are divided into seven levels. Which bracket you fall into and the rate you will pay depends on your annual taxable income as well as your filing status. There are four filing statuses, but we'll only focus on single filers and the first three tax brackets.

AGI	Tax rate
$0 to $11,000	10%
$11,001 to $44,725	12%
$44,726 to $95,375	22%

Figure 3 – Single Taxpayer Tax Brackets for 2023

The federal government uses a progressive income tax system, meaning the more you earn, the higher the percentage of taxes you pay. In this system, different portions of your income are taxed at different rates.

When filing a federal tax return, you have the option to either take a standard deduction or itemize your deductions. Itemizing may be beneficial for those with significant tax-deductible expenses, like mortgage interest or hefty medical bills. However, for simplicity, we'll focus on the standard deduction which in 2023 is $13,850 for single filers. This means if your annual income is less than $13,850, you owe no federal income tax. If you had federal taxes withheld from your paycheck, you would need to file a tax return to claim a refund. Keep in mind, though, that you might still owe state or local taxes.

As an example, let's say you earned $30,000 in 2023 and you file as a single filer; the standard deduction would be subtracted first to determine your taxable or adjusted gross income (AGI). In this example, your taxable income would be $16,150. The first $11,000 of your AGI would be taxed at 10% for a tax of $1,100.

The balance of $5,150 would be taxed at 12% and come to $618 because that chunk falls into the next tax bracket. You pay the higher tax only on the portion that falls within that bracket, not on the entire amount. The total income tax on $30,000 would be $1,100 + $618, which equals $1,718.

LOWERING YOUR TAXES

There are two primary ways to lower your taxes: through tax credits and tax deductions. In this book, we will focus mainly on tax credits, as most teens are likely to use the standard deduction.

Here are a few tax credits that you might qualify for:

- Earned Income Credit: This credit is available to most U.S. citizens and resident aliens earning less than $63,398, allowing them to claim at least a portion of this credit.
- Education Credit: You may be eligible for this if your parents do not claim you as a dependent and you have incurred qualified education expenses.
- Clean Vehicle Credit: This credit can be earned by purchasing a new or used vehicle that meets certain environmental standards.

Using these methods to reduce your taxes is entirely legal and is known as tax avoidance. However, it's important to distinguish this from tax evasion, which involves dishonest practices such as lying about your income or hiding information. Tax evasion is illegal and can result in severe penalties, including fines and jail time.

FILING A TAX RETURN

You may be wondering whether you need to file a tax return. Suppose your annual income is less than the standard deduction, which for 2023 is $13,850. In that case, you don't owe any federal taxes and typically wouldn't need to file a return. However, if you had federal income tax withheld during the year, you should file a return to receive a refund. Once your earnings exceed the standard deduction, you are required to start paying federal income taxes.

To file a tax return, you'll need specific documents depending on your type of income. Employees will receive a W-2 form from their employer, while independent contractors will get a 1099 from any person or business that paid them $600 or more. If you have other types of taxable income, you'll need the appropriate statements for those as well. Even if you don't receive these forms, you must report all your income. To calculate your federal tax liability, fill out Form 1040 and submit it to the IRS. This can be done anytime from January 1st until April 15th or the next business day if April 15th falls on a weekend or public holiday.

Remember, you also have to file a separate state return if your state has an income tax and a city return for those few cities that tax income. Of the states that tax income, 12 have a flat tax. The rest have a progressive tax similar to the federal system.

There are two ways to file your tax return – either by mail or online. Paper forms get processed more slowly than electronic ones, so if you're expecting a refund, it may take several months to arrive. Filing online yourself or with the help of a tax preparer is the most convenient way to file. I use a service called

FreeTaxUSA.com. It's my favorite online tax prep website for several reasons:

- It leads you step-by-step through the form so you don't miss any deductions you may be entitled to.
- There is no charge to file a federal tax return, and state returns are under $20.
- It retains all your information, so next year's return goes even faster.

Once you have filed your taxes, you may either owe money or be due a refund. If you owe money, follow the easy step-by-step process to pay online. If you are due a refund, you can request for it to be paid directly into your bank account. If you don't have one of those yet, don't worry. We'll cover that in one of the later chapters.

FinLit Fast Track

Action Steps

1. If you have never filed a tax return yourself, download a current form 1040 and practice filling it out. You can get it here: https://FinLitFastTrack.com/1040. You may also want the instructions that are here: https://FinLitFastTrack.com/1040-instructions.
2. There are many more taxes besides income taxes. Write down the ones you can think of, i.e. sales tax, then go to https://FinLitFastTrack.com/tax-type to see how many you got right. What are your thoughts about taxes after this exercise?

Questions

1. How does a clear understanding of income taxes benefit you as a responsible taxpayer?
2. Can you differentiate between tax evasion and tax avoidance, and why is it important to abide by tax laws?
3. How do you plan to continue your education on income taxes to stay informed about changes in tax laws and opportunities for deductions?
4. Have you shared what you've learned about income taxes with peers, family members, or friends, and what insights or questions emerged from these discussions?

Understanding and managing your tax obligations is a critical element of financial literacy, and you've taken significant steps toward becoming a more informed and responsible financial individual.

In the upcoming Part III, we'll focus on banking, budgeting, and spending. The next chapter delves into the fundamental aspects of banking, designed specifically with teens in mind. We're here to guide you through the process. Let's embark on this enlightening journey into the world of banking.

PART THREE

CHAPTER 5
NAVIGATING THE BANKING LANDSCAPE

A bank is a place where they lend you an umbrella in fair weather and ask for it back when it begins to rain.

ROBERT FROST, AMERICAN POET

This quote doesn't apply to all banks, but you should be careful which institutions you trust with your money. You can't really go your whole life without having a bank account; we all need one. However, you can make sure that you build a relationship with a good institution.

Banking is the cornerstone of financial management. Understanding the various types of banks, account options (such as checking and savings accounts), fees associated with banking services, and how to choose a financial institution is crucial for effective financial control and stability.

You might be wondering why a bank account is necessary, other than not having to carry cash around all the time. That's probably the first reason—the sheer convenience of just swiping your card when you need to pay for something. There are a few other reasons, such as the following:

1. **Easier transactions**: It's pretty difficult to buy something online without a bank account. Linking your card to online stores makes it much easier to complete purchases.

2. **You have peace of mind:** Keeping your money in a bank account gives you peace of mind that your money is safe. If you keep your cash in the house, there is a bigger possibility of theft, destruction through natural disasters, etc.

3. **Earning interest**: When you keep cash, nothing happens with it when you don't use it. If you keep your money in a bank account, the longer it stays in the account, the more interest you earn on the balance. The interest might be small, but it's money that you didn't have and wouldn't get if it wasn't deposited in a bank account.

4. **Promotions and perks:** Some banks offer exclusive promotions or reward programs when you have an account with them.

INS AND OUTS OF BANKING

There are many other benefits, but these will depend on the type of bank you decide to go with. The three main types of banks— retail banks, online banks, and credit unions—each offer unique banking experiences, catering to the different needs and preferences of their customers. They also have different account types, so it can become quite overwhelming to choose one. We'll briefly discuss each.

Retail Banks

Retail Banks are traditional brick-and-mortar institutions that offer a wide range of services, including checking and savings accounts, loans, and investment products. They have physical locations that customers can visit for in-person service. Retail banks are categorized further into National/Multinational banks like Wells Fargo and Citibank, smaller regional banks, and local banks that may only operate in a county or two. The main advantages of retail banks are their comprehensive service offerings and widespread accessibility. However, they often have higher fees and lower interest rates on savings compared to online banks and credit unions.

Online Banks

Online banks operate exclusively on the Internet and have no physical branches. This allows them to offer higher interest rates on deposits and lower fees, as they have lower overhead costs than traditional banks. Online banks are ideal for tech-savvy users who are comfortable managing their finances digitally. The downside is the lack of personal, face-to-face customer service and sometimes limited options for cash deposits.

Credit Unions

Credit Unions are member-owned nonprofit organizations, which often translates to more favorable rates and lower fees for their members. They tend to have a more community-focused approach, offering personalized customer service. Membership is typically based on specific affiliations like location, employer, or other community-based criteria. While they can offer a more personal banking experience and better rates, their technological offerings and geographic reach might be more limited compared to larger retail or online banks.

ACCOUNT TYPES

We'll examine choosing the right institution later, but let's first explore the different account options, their features, pros, and cons.

Checking Account

A checking account is a fundamental financial tool that allows you to deposit and withdraw money frequently, making it ideal for managing daily transactions. One significant advantage of having a checking account is the convenience it offers; you can quickly pay bills, receive direct deposits, and use debit cards for purchases.

Many checking accounts also provide online and mobile banking services, which help you monitor your finances and transfer money on the go. However, there are some disadvantages to consider. Checking accounts often come with various fees, which we will go over later in the chapter. Additionally, unlike savings accounts, most checking accounts offer little to no interest on your deposited funds, which means your money won't grow over time.

When you open a checking account, you have access to the following services:

- **Debit cards**: You can conveniently pay with your debit card without needing to draw cash from an ATM. A debit card gives you access to money that is already yours. Credit cards, on the other hand, are like taking loans from the bank. We will dive deeper into credit cards in Chapter 10.

- **ATMs**: ATMs do more than spit out cash. Most of them also allow you to deposit cash or checks, transfer money between your savings and checking accounts, and check your account balances. Some can even activate a new debit card, sell you a book of stamps, or even pay certain bills. Regardless of which branch you open your account at, you have access to any of your bank's ATMs for free.

- **Direct deposit**: This service allows anyone (including your employer or clients) to transfer money directly into your account for immediate access. This is a very convenient feature to take advantage of. Some employers may even let you split your check between checking and savings.

- **Online banking**: Most banks offer at least basic online banking. Besides checking your balances, online banking makes it easy to transfer money between accounts. The more robust versions will also offer bill pay and let you apply for a loan.

- **Banking app**: If your bank offers online banking, it most likely has an app, too. In addition to all the online banking features, the app lets you deposit checks by taking a photo of them. If your debit card is lost or stolen, you may be able to disable it so no one else can withdraw money or make purchases.

Savings Account

A savings account is a type of bank account where you can deposit money to earn interest over time. These accounts typically offer higher interest rates compared to checking accounts. While you can make withdrawals from a savings account, there might be limits on how many you can make each month. Additionally, maintaining a minimum balance may be necessary to avoid monthly fees. Some banks also offer the option to automatically transfer funds from your savings to cover any overdrafts on your checking account. However, access to funds directly via a debit card may only be available with some savings accounts.

There are various types of savings accounts that you can choose from. Here are the most popular ones:

- **Traditional savings account**: This is the most common type of savings account and is a low-risk savings option.
- **Student savings account**: This is similar to a traditional savings account; however, it is designed especially for teens and may offer perks not available on other accounts.
- **Christmas club**: This is a savings account in which you deposit money regularly throughout the year and only access it for the holiday season. It's a fantastic way to avoid paying for holiday shopping with your credit card.
- **Certificate of Deposit (CD):** This is a hybrid savings/investment account that pays a higher interest

rate. The tradeoff is that you cannot access your money for a set period, typically between six months and five years. Ideally, the longer the "investment" period, the higher the interest rate.

NAVIGATING BANKING CHARGES

Every account comes with some banking charges and/or fees. Knowing how to minimize or avoid them will give you a financial advantage and help you spend your money on the things you really want instead of giving it to the bank.

Monthly Account Fee

Many banks impose a monthly account fee to cover administrative costs associated with maintaining your account. However, there are often ways to avoid these fees, and it's advisable to inquire about them before opening an account. Common methods to waive this fee include:

- Setting up a monthly direct deposit.
- Opening both a checking and savings account with the same bank.
- Maintaining a minimum monthly balance.

For students, many banks offer accounts without a monthly fee, making them an excellent option to consider.

Out-Of-Network ATM Fee

Using an ATM outside your bank's network can result in additional charges, including a fee from your bank and another from the ATM owner. While these fees might seem minor for a single transaction, they can accumulate over time. To avoid these costs, try to use ATMs within your bank's network. Some banks offer a perk of reimbursing these fees up to a certain amount each month, so it's worth asking about this feature when choosing a bank. If you find yourself in a situation where you must use an out-of-network ATM, consider withdrawing enough cash to avoid needing multiple transactions.

Non-sufficient Fund Fee

Non-sufficient funds (NSF) fees, also known as bounced check fees, occur when you attempt to make a payment but don't have enough money in your account to cover the transaction. When this happens, the bank can either decline the transaction or cover the payment on your behalf, which leads to an overdraft. NSF fees are charged for each transaction that the bank declines due to insufficient funds and can be quite costly (up to $35 per transaction).

Overdraft Fee

Overdraft fees are incurred when your bank covers a payment that exceeds the balance in your account, essentially allowing your balance to go negative. This can be a helpful service in a pinch, but it comes at a cost. Overdraft fees can quickly add up, especially if multiple transactions are covered by the bank in this way. Some banks offer overdraft protection services, which may link your checking account to a savings account, credit card, or line of credit to cover any shortfalls.

To avoid NSF and overdraft fees, consider setting up alerts with your bank to notify you when your balance is low. Also, regularly review your account balances and upcoming bills to ensure you have sufficient funds to cover all your expenses. Some banks also offer apps that can help you track your spending and avoid overdrafts and NSF fees.

Early Account Closing Fee

When you want to close your account, most banks require a notice period of between 90 and 180 days, during which your account will still be active, and you will be liable for any fees associated with it. If you want to close your account early, you will need to pay an early account closing fee.

Before closing your account, read the terms and conditions and choose whatever makes the most sense for you. If closing it will cost less, that will be the best action to take. Alternatively, you might find it cheaper to keep the account for the notice period.

Other Bank Services

Besides keeping your money safe, banks offer a variety of other services that you probably won't utilize until you're older. Some of these offerings are:

- Loans for vehicles, boats, campers, and other large purchases
- Home loans (mortgages) and home equity lines of credit (HELOC)
- Signature loans and personal lines of credit
- Money orders and cashier's checks
- Notary services
- Investment advising

- Money wiring
- Services specifically for businesses

CHOOSING A BANKING INSTITUTION

When choosing a bank, keep in mind that, ideally, you're looking for a long-term partner who can assist you with every phase of your financial life. As a minor teen, you may also get additional protection and features that adults may not have access to. This includes parental control or oversight, so you don't have to worry about the details, extra fraud protection, parental notifications, lower fees (if any), additional financial education, and age-appropriate access to your account. This means that all the complex tasks are left to your parents.

Here are some tips on how to choose the right bank for you.

- **Choose your account type**: This could influence the institution you choose since not all institutions offer the same account types.
- **Consider the digital features**: Some banks are more technologically advanced in terms of what they offer members than others. Look for a bank that provides the best digital features to meet your current and potential future needs.
- **Local branches**: If you're going with a retail bank, make sure that you have a local branch in your area. It's always easier to resolve matters in person than over the phone or online.
- **Look at the fees**: Some banks charge lower fees than others for the same account type. Look for the bank with the lowest cost for your chosen account type. Beware of

any possible hidden fees, such as transaction and withdrawal fees.

- **Read the terms and conditions**: Before you open an account, make sure that you understand the terms and conditions applicable to the account. Ask an adult to go over these terms and conditions with you.
- **Consider a credit union**: Although these are restricted to certain people, try to look for one you qualify for. Many have loosened their member criteria in the last decade. They provide most, if not all, of the same services as banks.

OPENING A BANK ACCOUNT

Once you know where you want to open your account and what type of account you want, it's time to gather some documents.

To open a bank account, you need the following:

- A government-issued ID, if you have one
- a Social Security number
- Proof of address – if your ID doesn't include your current one
- A parent to authorize the account if you're under 18 or you don't have ID.
- Most importantly: money!

You may be able to open your account online. If not, call the bank for an appointment so you don't have to wait in line. In either case, you will have to fill out and sign several forms. The whole process will take about an hour. If you open your account in person, many banks can issue your debit card immediately. If that isn't an option, expect to receive your debit card by mail, typically within two weeks.

FinLit Fast Track

Activities

1. Open your first bank account. Follow the guidelines in this chapter to choose a bank and gather the documents listed above. Download and fill out the banking worksheet from https://FinLitFastTrack.com/banking to help you decide. Open your account online or visit a local branch with a parent.

Banking is the heart of your financial life, and you've acquired essential knowledge to manage your finances effectively and conveniently.

In the upcoming chapter, we will focus on budgeting and spending, two crucial components of financial success. You'll learn how to create a budget that aligns with your financial goals, track your spending, and make informed decisions about where your money goes.

CHAPTER 6
FINANCIAL FREEDOM BEGINS HERE: BUDGETING AND SMART SPENDING

" *Unless you control your money, making more won't help. You'll just have bigger payments.*

DAVE RAMSEY, FINANCIAL ADVISOR
AND RADIO HOST

Budgeting often gets a bad rap. Some people think it's just a way to restrict spending and cut out all the fun. But actually, the opposite is true. A budget isn't just about preventing over-spending—it's about making sure there's enough money for both necessities and fun. Budgeting can indeed feel limiting, but it also offers a lot of freedom by letting you know exactly how much money you can spend without worry.

It's often those who feel they don't have much money who resist budgeting the most. However, the real beauty of a budget lies in its ability to show you precisely where your money is going. It keeps surprises at bay, like forgotten bills that suddenly pop up just when you think you have extra money to spend. Without a budget, it's too easy to overlook these expenses, leading to stress and financial strain. But with a budget, you can breathe a sigh of relief, knowing that you have a plan in place to manage your money.

One common reason we overspend is due to FOMO—the fear of missing out. We worry about being left out or skipping experiences that might not come around again, which can lead to poor financial choices. This feeling is widespread; research by Anwar et al. (2020) found that 55% of teens between 15 and 18 years old experience FOMO.

But here's the thing: I'm a huge advocate for budgeting. It has significantly improved my financial life, allowing me to achieve goals and maintain control over my money. Creating a budget, tracking your expenses, and making thoughtful spending decisions can help you optimize your resources and build financial stability. And you're not alone in this—according to Maurie Backman (2017), about 40% of teens are already making wise financial choices by sticking to a budget. So, when you budget, you're in good company and far from boring—you're taking charge of your financial future.

BUDGETING BASICS

One fantastic thing a budget does is help your money to go further. You think twice before making impulse decisions. If you think back to our twins in the introduction, David never budgeted and was always in a pickle with his finances. Emma loved to budget, and she made smart spending decisions. In doing so, she always had enough money to do what she wanted to when the opportunity arose. This is the power of smart spending-it allows you to make the most of your money and enjoy the things that truly matter to you.

Budget Worksheet   **Month:**   *May*

Income

Source	Budgeted	Actual	Difference
job	$408	$414.98	$6.98
allowance	$80	$80.00	$0
gifts	$0	$50.00	$50.00
	$488	$544.98	$56.98

Expenses

Category	Budgeted	Actual	Difference
savings	$75	$100	$25.00
insurance	$50	$50	$0
gas	$100	$97.33	($2.67)
cellphone	$35	$35	$0
food	$75	$73.26	($1.74)
clothes	$40	$44.92	$4.92
fun	$45	$54.14	$9.14
donations	$25	$40	$15.00
miscellaneous	$43	$45.23	$2.23
	$488	$539.88	$51.88

Figure 4 – Emma's Budget Worksheet

Figure 4 is an example of Emma's budget. Notice that her income for May was more than she anticipated because she won a $50 gift card in a school raffle. But instead of blowing the entire amount, she wisely put half of it in savings. She also exceeded her budget in two categories but still stayed within her budget because she spent less on others. What she didn't spend in May, she can add to her

June budget, put more in savings, or treat herself to something special. The point is she has choices because she sticks to her budget!

A budget consists of four main elements: income, expenses, debt, and savings. By categorizing your financial activity into these four areas, you can create a clear and effective budget that helps maintain financial stability and achieve your long-term financial goals.

Income: The foundation of your budget is your income. Before you plan your spending, tally up all sources of income you expect to receive, such as wages, allowances, birthday money, and interest from investments. This total will dictate how you allocate funds across the rest of your budget.

Expenses: Distinguish your spending between fixed and variable expenses:

- **Fixed Expenses**: These are the non-negotiable monthly costs that you must meet, such as phone bills, subscription services, and, eventually, recurring essentials like rent, utilities, and groceries.
- **Variable Expenses**: These costs fluctuate and include items such as clothing, dining out, and entertainment. Allocate funds to these expenses only after covering your fixed expenses, debt payments, and savings contributions.
- **Debt**: This typically includes secured debts such as a car loan, which are part of your fixed expenses. You might also have unsecured debts, like credit card debt, that need careful management.
- **Savings**: Building savings is an integral part of budgeting, which will be discussed in detail in Chapter

7. Consistently setting aside money in a savings account helps secure your financial future and prepare for unexpected expenses.

Creating a budget might seem complex, but understanding the correct categories to include can simplify the process. Here are six easy steps to help you make a budget. You can also download a budget worksheet from https://FinLitFastTrack.com/budget to guide you through these steps.

1. **Calculate Your Income**: Start by figuring out how much money you make each month. If your income varies, it's crucial to update your budget regularly to reflect these changes.

2. **List All Your Expenses:** First, jot down all your essential expenses—these are your non-negotiables like transportation, food, and any recurring bills. Next, list variable expenses such as birthday gifts or occasional treats, which might not occur every month. Don't forget to include categories for savings and any debts you're paying off.

3. **Allocate Income to Expenses**: Divide your expenses into needs (essential expenses and debts) and wants (everything else). Allocate your income to cover your needs first. Whatever is left can go towards your wants, like entertainment or eating out.

4. **Track Your Spending:** Use the budget worksheet to monitor your expenses throughout the month. Record every purchase, no matter how small—it all adds up. Aim to stay within the limits you've set for each category.

5. **Adjust as Needed:** The first few months are often about trial and error. You might not know how much you spend on casual outings off the bat, but by the third month, you should start to see

patterns and can adjust your budget more accurately. Make it a habit to review and tweak your budget monthly based on your spending habits and financial goals.

By following these steps and using a budget worksheet, you can gain better control over your finances, ensure you're covering all your expenses, and start saving for your future.

BUDGETING TOOLS AND STRATEGIES

If you don't want to use the spreadsheet, there are a few budgeting apps that are worth considering. The following apps are ones that stand out as being good for teens, but there are many others on the market for you to choose from.

- **Goodbudget**: Both the free and paid versions offer the same features, although the free version limits you to 20 "envelopes." This should be more than enough for the average teen.
- **EveryDollar**: Dave Ramsey's app includes extensive financial education. If you'd like to keep learning beyond this book, it's worth trying. The downside is the free version doesn't include synching with your bank, and the paid version may be too expensive for a teen to afford. If your parents will cover the cost, then that won't be an issue.
- **Simplifi**: This app was developed by Quicken, the maker of the popular accounting software QuickBooks, so you know it has value. They don't offer a free version, but the paid version is under $5.00 a month.

In addition to using apps and worksheets, there are several strategic approaches you can adopt to budget more effectively. We'll explore three popular strategies: Paying Yourself First, Zero-Based Budgeting, and the 50/30/20 Rule.

Pay Yourself First

This approach prioritizes saving over all other expenses. Before you pay your bills or spend on other needs, you set aside a predetermined amount for savings—this could be for an emergency fund, retirement, or a specific financial goal. By doing this, you ensure that you're consistently building your savings. Often, people do the opposite: they only save what's left after all other expenses, which can result in saving very little or nothing at all. Paying yourself first helps you rethink your spending priorities and cut down on unnecessary expenses.

Zero-Based Budgeting

Zero-based budgeting involves assigning every dollar of your income to a specific expense so that your total income minus your total expenses equals zero at the end of the month. This doesn't mean you blow all your money on shopping; instead, any leftover funds should be directed toward paying off debt or boosting your savings. This method is excellent for debt repayment and saving, and it teaches you to manage your finances tightly, ensuring you don't spend more than you make.

50/30/20 Rule

This rule helps you to categorize your spending and saving. According to this strategy, you should allocate 50% of your income to essential needs, 30% to wants, and 20% to savings. This framework can be adjusted based on your specific financial situation and goals. Still, it provides a clear guideline for balancing your budget. It's straightforward but can be challenging to implement, especially if your expenses don't neatly fit into these categories.

These strategies offer different approaches to managing your money, and you might find one more suitable than the others based on your personal financial situation. Experiment with them to find out which method helps you achieve your financial goals most effectively.

SMART SPENDING

Adopting healthy and smart spending habits is essential to making a budget truly effective. Setting a budget is one thing; changing your spending behaviors is another. If you continue spending as you did before setting a budget, you'll likely see little improvement in your financial situation.

For many of us, online shopping is a big temptation, especially with ads that seem to know exactly what we want when we want it. Here are some strategies to help you spend smarter and stick to your budget:

1. **Compare Prices**: Always check if the item you want is available at a lower price elsewhere. Use online tools and apps like price.com to help you compare prices easily.
2. **Avoid Payment Plans**: Unless it's a significant purchase (which we'll discuss later), avoid buying in installments. Payment plans often come with interest,

making the item more expensive over time. It's better to save up and pay in full.

3. **Unsubscribe from Marketing Emails:** To resist temptation, unsubscribe from marketing emails. Often, stores will send promotions that can lead to impulse buys. You can usually find the unsubscribe option at the bottom of the email. Remember to opt out of marketing communications when making online purchases.

4. **Create a Splurge Fund:** Within your budget, set aside a small amount for unplanned purchases. This allows you some flexibility to buy something special without derailing your financial plans. Stick strictly to this predetermined amount.

5. **Implement the 24-Hour Rule:** If you find something you want but haven't budgeted for, wait 24 hours before buying. This pause can help you decide if it's really worth buying or just an impulse. If you still believe it's a worthwhile purchase after a day, consider how to responsibly add it to your budget.

6. **Remove Saved Credit Card Information**: Don't store your credit card information on websites. Having to enter your details manually each time adds an extra step that can make you think twice about unnecessary purchases.

7. **Steer Clear of Bundle Deals**: Bundle deals, like buy-two-get-one-free, can seem like a bargain, but they often lead you to buy more than you need. Unless you genuinely need every item in the offer, skip these deals to avoid spending on things you don't need.

By applying these intelligent spending strategies, you can gain better control over your finances and make sure your budget works effectively for you. A final point to consider, whether you're shopping online or in-store, is the importance of curbing impulse purchases. These are often the culprits that cause us to exceed our budget. While resisting a seemingly irresistible deal or the strong urge to buy can be challenging, here's a helpful mnemonic —CHANGE—to guide you during those tempting moments:

- **C for Cost**: Consider the true cost of the item. It's not just about the price tag but also what you might have to sacrifice in your budget to accommodate this purchase, like cutting back on savings.
- **H for Happiness**: Reflect on the joy this item will bring. Is it a fleeting pleasure, or will it provide lasting satisfaction? Often, the excitement over something new fades quickly.
- **A for Affordability**: Ask yourself if you can genuinely afford the item. If purchasing it strains your budget or puts you in debt, it's wise to pass.
- **N for Need**: Evaluate the necessity of the purchase. Do you really need it, or could you do without it? If it's not essential, think twice before buying.
- **G for Gain**: Consider what you gain from this purchase. Is it for personal satisfaction, or are you trying to impress others? Make sure your reasons align with your personal values.
- **E for Elsewhere**: Think about whether your money could be better spent on another area of your budget. Could these funds fulfill a more pressing need or long-term goal?

By keeping the CHANGE acronym in mind, you can strengthen your decision-making process and keep your spending in check.

This approach helps ensure that every purchase you make is thoughtful and contributes positively to your financial well-being.

FinLit Fast Track

Activities

1. If you have trouble with impulse spending, brainstorm some ways to help you break the habit. I once knew someone who kept her credit card frozen in a bowl of ice. Her logic was, by the time it thawed out, the urge to buy would have passed. What are some things you could do to make you stop the next time you are tempted to buy something that isn't in your budget?
2. Create your budget – Start by tracking all of your expenses for an entire month. Remembering to get a receipt every time you buy something will make this easier. Once the month has passed, use the information to set up a budget using the worksheet from FinLit Fast Track (https://FinLitFastTrack.com/budget) or a budgeting app. Remember to adapt as needed until you have a stable budget. Every month will be different, but certain things will remain constant throughout.

Questions

Here are some questions to reflect on when building a personal budget.

1. Have I made provision for unexpected expenses?
2. Does my income match my expenses?

3. If my expenses are higher than my income, where can I cut down on costs?
4. Does my budget support my financial goals?
5. Can I do anything to increase my income?
6. What can I learn from this month's spending to improve next month?
7. Do I have any debt, and am I paying enough toward it?

You learned how to create a budget that aligns with your financial goals, track your expenses, and make informed spending decisions.

Part IV focuses on building wealth and financial security through saving and investing. In the upcoming chapter, we'll explore the world of saving and compounding interest.

PART FOUR

CHAPTER 7
SMART SAVINGS STARTS HERE

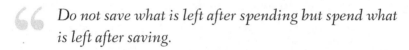

Do not save what is left after spending but spend what is left after saving.

WARREN BUFFET, CEO OF BERKSHIRE HATHAWAY

This quote echoes the "Pay yourself first" principle introduced in Chapter 6, an incredibly potent yet often overlooked strategy. This approach is not merely about saving for specific goals like vacations or big purchases. It is particularly beneficial for building your emergency fund and retirement savings.

You might think you're too young to start considering retirement, but that's not the case. The earlier you begin, the better your financial future looks. I've encountered people in their early 50s who haven't saved anything for retirement and now believe it's too late to start. Developing a habit of saving from a young age is essential for long-term financial stability.

Starting at an early age isn't just about forming good habits. It allows you to leverage the power of compounding interest, enhances your investment management skills, helps you correct any financial misconceptions from your upbringing, and teaches you how to effectively manage financial risks. These benefits make a compelling case for beginning your savings journey as soon as possible.

SIMPLE VS. COMPOUND INTEREST

Compound interest is especially powerful for growing your savings, particularly from a young age. It involves earning interest on your interest, meaning that each month, your interest earnings are added to your principal, allowing future interest calculations to be based on a larger amount. This process accelerates the growth of your savings exponentially over time. The longer your money is invested, the bigger the advantage.

Simple interest, on the other hand, is more straightforward. It's calculated as a fixed amount on the original principal alone, regardless of any interest earned. For example, if you invest $200 with a monthly interest rate of 1% (12% annually), you will earn a consistent $2.00 every month. After five years, which totals 60 months, you will have earned $120 in interest, bringing your overall balance to $320.

Let's compare this with compound interest using the same initial investment of $200 at a 1% compounded monthly. In this scenario, each month's interest is added to the principal before the next

month's interest calculation, resulting in significantly more significant growth over the same period.

- For the first month, the calculation will be the same as
  before, and you will earn $2.00 in interest.
- For the second month, the starting balance is $202.00,
  and 1% of it will be $2.02, bringing the total after the
  second month to $204.02.
- For the third month, the starting balance is $204.02, and
  1% of it will be $2.04, bringing the total after the third
  month to $206.06.
- This principle is repeated for the 60 months.
- After 60 months, you have earned $152.47 in interest,
  bringing your total balance to $352.47.

Viewing compound interest on a monthly basis might not seem
impressive, but its cumulative effect on your savings is remarkable.
In the previously mentioned example, using compound interest
earned an additional $32.47 over simple interest in just five years.
Now, imagine the impact over more extended periods, such as 10
or 20 years. To illustrate, if that $200 were allowed to grow for 20
years, the total balance with compound interest would reach
$1,929.26, compared to only $680 with simple interest. What a
difference!

To determine how long it will take for your money to double, you
can use the rule of 72. Divide 72 by the annual compound interest
rate. For example, if the annual interest rate is 5%, it will take over
14 years to double your investment ($72/5 = 14.4$).

Simple vs. Compound Interest

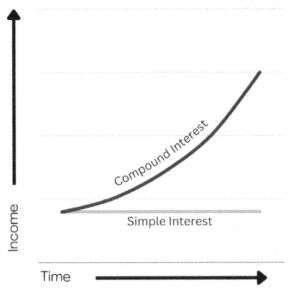

Figure 5 - Interest Over Time

You can take advantage of the power of compound interest in the following ways:

- **Start early**: You've seen the difference above between investing for 5 years vs. 20 years. The earlier you start, the more you will get out!
- **Save consistently**: Try to add more to the savings/investment as often as you can so that there is a bigger base to earn interest from. The more you add, the more interest you will receive, and the more it will compound over time.

CULTIVATING THE HABIT OF SAVING

Developing strong saving habits early on is crucial. Here are some effective strategies:

- Pay Yourself First: Always prioritize setting aside a portion of your income into savings. Make savings the top category in your budget.
- Automate Savings: Use your banks transfer feature to move money to your savings accounts automatically when you receive your income.
- Accelerate Your Plan: Always put a portion of unexpected income in savings.

Setting SMART Financial Goals

One of the most effective ways for teens to approach saving money is by setting SMART financial goals. SMART stands for Specific, Measurable, Achievable, Relevant, and Time-bound. This framework helps clarify your objectives and increases the likelihood of achieving them. For instance, instead of vaguely deciding to save for a new video game, a SMART goal would be, "I will save $60 for the new 'Zelda' game by saving $10 each week for the next six weeks." This goal is specific (saving for 'Zelda'), measurable ($60), achievable ($10 per week isn't too high a sum), relevant (it's a game you really want), and time-bound (six weeks).

Start with short-term goals like saving for a day at the water park park or a new outfit, and then gradually work up to long-term goals such as saving for a car or college expenses. This method not only makes the process of saving more systematic but also more rewarding as you tick off goals one by one. Setting and achieving financial goals during your teen years can build a solid foundation for more complex financial planning in adulthood.

Rewards for Reaching Savings Milestones

To make saving money more engaging, consider setting up a rewards system to help you reach your savings milestones. Just as businesses often reward loyal customers, you can reward yourself for diligent saving. For example, suppose your goal is to save $1000 for a top-of-the-line bike. In that case, you might treat yourself to a movie night after saving the first $400, then perhaps a meal out at your favorite restaurant at the $700 mark. These rewards provide additional motivation and a sense of accomplishment that makes the journey towards your financial goal enjoyable.

It's essential to ensure that these rewards are reasonable and don't counteract your saving efforts. Choose low-cost or meaningful rewards that enhance your savings experience without significantly detracting from your goal. This approach not only makes the process of saving more enjoyable but also ingrains the habit of associating financial discipline with positive outcomes, setting a pattern that can promote lifelong monetary health.

BUILDING AN EMERGENCY FUND

An emergency fund is critical for covering unexpected expenses without disrupting your financial stability. Start by defining what qualifies as an emergency to prevent misuse of these funds for non-essential expenses. Examples of emergencies are expensive, unexpected car repairs or replacing a stolen iPhone. A last-minute weekend trip to the beach doesn't qualify as an emergency. Sorry.

A good target for your emergency fund is to cover three to six months of expenses, providing a cushion during financial uncertainties.

Steps to Build Your Emergency Fund:

- **Assess Your Expenses**: Calculate your monthly spending to understand how much you need to save.
- **Set Achievable Goals:** Break your savings target into smaller, manageable goals to avoid feeling overwhelmed.
- **Separate Savings Account:** Consider setting up a dedicated account for your emergency fund and automating transfers to steadily build up your savings.

By understanding these principles and applying these strategies, you'll not only secure your current financial needs but also build a robust foundation for your future.

We've discussed various types of savings accounts, and you might wonder why it's necessary to have different ones. Each type of savings account is designed for specific purposes, depending on what you're saving for, whether it's something in the near future or a long-term goal. Let's break down why these different accounts are helpful:

Short-Term Savings:

Short-term savings are for upcoming expenses or purchases, like a new gadget, birthday gifts, or a holiday trip. Once you reach your saving target for a particular item, you can pause or redirect your contributions.

Long-Term Savings:

Long-term savings are used for bigger goals that are further in the future, like buying a car or saving for college. You should continue to contribute to this account until you are close to achieving your goal, adjusting the contributions as needed based on changes in your income.

Emergency Fund:

An emergency fund is essential for financial security. It is designed to cover unexpected expenses such as urgent car repairs or medical bills. As already stated, this fund should cover three to six months of expenses, providing a financial cushion in emergencies. Once this fund reaches its goal, you can stop contributing to it until you need to use it, in which case you should replenish it afterward.

Is It Necessary to Have Different Physical Accounts?

Yes, it can be beneficial to manage your savings by keeping them in separate accounts for each goal. This organization helps prevent you from spending money reserved for emergencies on non-essential items. It makes it easier to track your progress toward each goal. Additionally, different accounts may offer specific features suited to their purpose—such as higher interest for long-term savings or more liquidity for short-term needs.

By understanding and utilizing different types of savings accounts, you can effectively manage your finances and ensure that you are prepared for both immediate needs and future goals. This structured approach to saving can help you achieve financial stability and peace of mind.

FinLit Fast Track

Activities

1. If you don't already have a savings account, open one now. Look back to the chapter on banking and review how to choose a bank that is right for you.

2. Ask your parents to start a cash-match pact: If you have a bad track record with saving, your parents might jump at this opportunity. This pact requires them to match whatever you manage to save. If you save $10 for the month, they have to match it. It's an easy way to double your savings.

3. Set a savings goal – either a percentage of your income or a set dollar amount. Determine how much you want to have in your account at the end of one year. Write out this statement and put it where you can see it often:

> *On or before (date), I will have (amount) in my savings account.*

4. Play with the compound interest calculator at https://FinLitFastTrack.com/compounding to get excited about saving.

The 52-Week Money-Saving Challenge

The 52-week money-saving challenge cultivates a habit of saving by forcing you to regularly put away a set amount for a whole year. It doesn't always have to be $1 increments. You can adapt the amount based on your income. Commit to saving 50 cents or even 25 cents per week. Alternatively, you can also change it from weekly to bi-weekly. Find a method and amount that works for you and commit to it.

The easiest way to do this is to get a jar and a notebook. You can use the one below or create your own template in your notebook and track your progress. Remember to go up to week 52 and not stop at week 5 like I did! When you've placed the amount in the jar, you can highlight the line or cross it off. This is also a great way to start your emergency fund!

Week	Amount	Total
1	$0.50	$0.50
2	$1.00	$1.50
3	$1.50	$3.00
4	$2.00	$5.00
5	$2.50	$7.50

Questions

1. What are your thoughts on the "pay yourself first" principle?
2. Can you explain the difference between simple and compound interest?
3. What method do you plan to use to hit your savings goal?

You learned the importance of saving, setting financial goals, and how compounding interest can multiply your wealth over time.

In the upcoming chapter, we'll journey into the exciting realm of investing. You'll explore different investment options, understand risk and return, and discover the strategies for growing your wealth.

MAKE A DIFFERENCE WITH YOUR REVIEW
UNLOCK THE POWER OF GENEROSITY

"As we work to create light for others, we naturally light our own way."

MARY ANN RADMACHER

People who give without expectation live longer, happier lives, and make more money. If we've got a shot at that during our time together, let's give it a try.

To make that happen, I have a question for you...

Would you help someone you've never met, even if you never got credit for it?

Who is this person, you ask? They are like you. Or, at least, like you used to be. Less experienced, wanting to make a difference, and needing help, but not sure where to look.

My mission is to make financial literacy accessible to all teens. Everything I do stems from that mission. And the only way for me to accomplish that mission is by reaching...well...everyone.

This is where you come in. Most people do, in fact, judge a book by its cover (and its reviews). So, here's my ask on behalf of a struggling teen you've never met:

Please help that teen by leaving this book a review.

Your gift costs no money and less than 60 seconds to make real but can change a fellow teen's life forever. Your review could help...

- ...one more student manage their money wisely.
- ...one more young adult save for their dreams.
- ...one more teenager feel confident about their financial future.
- ...one more peer make informed decisions.
- ...one more dream come true.

To get that 'feel good' feeling and help this person for real, all you have to do is...and it takes less than 60 seconds...leave a review.

Simply scan the QR code below to leave your review:

If you feel good about helping a faceless teen, you are my kind of person. Welcome to the club. You're one of us.

I'm that much more excited to help you achieve financial success faster, easier, and more confidently than you can possibly imagine. You'll love the strategies and lessons I'm about to share in the coming chapters.

Thank you from the bottom of my heart. Now, back to our regularly scheduled programming.

- Your biggest fan, Holly Sherman

PS - Fun fact: If you provide something of value to another person, it makes you more valuable to them. If you'd like goodwill straight from another teen - and you believe this book will help them - send this book their way.

CHAPTER 8
BUILDING YOUR FINANCIAL FUTURE

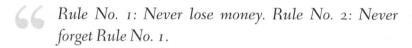 *Rule No. 1: Never lose money. Rule No. 2: Never forget Rule No. 1.*

WARREN BUFFETT, CEO OF BERKSHIRE HATHAWAY

Investments can be complex and high-risk. When I was younger, just hearing about investments would have me running in the opposite direction. Little did I know how powerful they could be. They're such a fantastic tool for achieving financial growth if you know what you're doing. There's a massive balance between risk and reward.

Let's cover the basics first.

To invest means to commit money to buying assets, hoping that they will increase in value over time. There are many reasons why people choose to invest, including for tax savings, for retirement, to protect themselves against inflation, for passive income, and to generate wealth.

Although there are many reasons why people invest, there are two primary outcomes they are looking for - either for the assets to appreciate in value or to return an income.

When you invest for income, you receive regular payments from your investment, usually monthly or every few months. One common way to do this is through real estate investments, where you earn income by renting out your property for more than your monthly mortgage payment and other expenses. Other options for income-generating investments include dividend-paying stocks, preferred stocks, and annuities. While the main goal is to generate income, it's also possible for the value of your asset to increase over time, giving you the potential for both income and capital appreciation.

Investing for appreciation involves buying assets in the hope that their value will increase over time, allowing you to sell them at a higher price later on. This type of investment is typically long-term, meaning you will see the benefits in the future. For example, real estate that you hold for many years and then sell for a profit is an appreciating asset. Stocks and commodities like copper and oil are also considered investments for capital appreciation. Investing for income and capital appreciation are not always mutually exclusive; you can benefit from both. Knowing which one you want to focus on will help you choose the types of assets you want to invest in.

There are two main types of assets that you can invest in, each offering multiple investments. You can either focus on paper assets such as stocks, bonds, EFTs, mutual funds, and treasury notes or real assets like cryptocurrency, real estate, precious metals, and art and collectibles. Let's look at the pros and cons to weigh up our options:

PAPER ASSETS

+ *Pros:*

- Easy to Buy and Sell: You can quickly turn paper assets into cash, making them super convenient if you need money fast.
- Mix it Up: With paper assets, you can invest in lots of different things—different companies, industries, or even countries. This helps spread out the risk.
- Easy to Start: You don't need a lot of money to start investing, which makes them an excellent choice for beginners.
- Earn money Regularly: Many paper assets can earn you money regularly through dividends (a share of the company's profit) or interest.

− *Cons:*

- Prices Jump Around: The value of paper assets can change a lot and quickly, which means they can be risky, and you might lose money, especially in the short term.
- Can Be Complicated: There's a lot to learn about paper assets and how they work, and it can be tricky to understand all the details.
- Losing Value Over Time: Sometimes, the value of paper assets doesn't keep up with inflation, which means they might buy less in the future than they do now.

REAL ASSETS

+ *Pros:*

- They're Real: You can see and touch real assets like buildings and gold. They also tend to hold their value over time, especially when prices are rising.
- Not Tied to the Stock Market: Real assets often don't follow the stock market's ups and downs, which can help protect your money when stocks are not doing well.
- Can Grow in Value: Some real assets, like houses, can increase in value over time, and if you rent them out, you can make money regularly.

− *Cons:*

- Harder to Sell Quickly: Unlike paper assets, real assets can take a long time to sell, and you might not get your money back as quickly as you'd like.
- Costs More to Start: Buying real assets can cost more upfront than buying paper assets. For example, buying a house is more expensive than buying a few shares of a company.
- Needs Ongoing Attention: Some real assets need to be taken care of. A house needs repairs, and collectibles and precious metals need to be stored.

INVESTING FOR BEGINNERS

Regardless of the type of asset you choose, there will always be a risk associated with the investment. By investing, we're hoping that the reward outweighs the risk. In simple terms, risk is the possibility that you might lose some or all of the money you invested. Reward is the financial return you get from the investment.

You might think that it's a no-brainer—don't take on too much risk but still get a reward. That's not terrible advice, but when it comes to investing, the greater the risk is, the bigger the reward will be. The problem is that the reward is never guaranteed. This is why so many people shy away from investing, but it really can be the best way to grow your money if you can get it right.

Before you decide to jump off a building with a promise to fly (figuratively speaking, of course), I think it's vital that we look at the best ways to balance risk and reward. Investing is not something you can jump into, like saving. You need to do a fair amount of planning and research before you invest. To make things a little easier, here are a few steps you can follow:

1. Educate yourself: Learning the basics of investing is the first step. This chapter should give you a good introduction, but there is much more to learn. Once you have the basics down, you can start with smaller investments and build your portfolio as you build on your experience.

2. Try mock portfolios first: There are quite a few apps out there where you can buy stocks and assets with fake money to gain some experience. You can set up a dummy trading portfolio to get the feel of how it works, and how to balance risk and reward. We'll look at some of these in the activity portion of this chapter.

3. Ask for professional advice: Financial professionals review and watch investments for a living. If you're feeling unsure or a little overwhelmed, consult with a

financial professional for some advice. It's their job to give you sound financial advice to protect your money.

4. Diversify your portfolio: This simply means not putting all your eggs in one basket. When looking at investment options, you want to have a good combination of different investments. For example, if you buy stock, you want to invest in different industries or sectors. Filling your portfolio only with gaming or E.V. manufacturer stocks, for example, is not a smart move. You may also want to add gold and silver coins, a collectible or two, and some real estate. It will obviously take some time to build this up, and you'll start with one, but keep diversity in mind as you build your portfolio.

5. Know what your risk tolerance is: Risk tolerance is the amount of risk you're willing to accept. We all have different risk tolerances. Some people can accept more risk, while others prefer to play it safe. Take some time to reflect on this. Your risk tolerance may also be influenced by how much you have to spend. When investing, you need to invest with the mindset that you might lose it all. So, never invest the money that you need for daily expenses.

6. Research, research, research: The value of investments can literally change overnight. Always make sure that you stay up to date with current information and trends to stay caught up and continue to profit. Regularly consult reliable resources like Yahoo Finance.

7. Reassess and rebalance when needed: By keeping an eye on the investment market, you will know when things change and when it's time to reevaluate your investments. You may need to make regular changes to

your investments to ensure they remain profitable
for you.

INVESTMENT OPTIONS

The following section is dedicated to exploring some of the assets
you can invest in. We will look at some paper assets first and then
review some real assets. This is not an all-inclusive guide but
should be used as a guideline for further research.

Paper Assets

Stocks

When you buy a share of common stock, you are purchasing a
small part of the company that is traded on an exchange like the
New York Stock Exchange. There are several exchanges in the
United States, and most other developed countries have their own.
To get on an exchange, a company must "go public" with an IPO
or initial public offering. This happens when the original investors
want to raise more money to expand the business or to recoup
some of their investment. At this point, the company's dealings are
subject to oversight by the Securities and Exchange Commission
(SEC).

Stocks are bought from brokers either using an online trading platform or a financial advisor. Schwab, Fidelity, and Robinhood are
just three examples of where you can purchase shares. Every stock
has a unique ticker symbol that differentiates it from all other
companies. For example, Apple's symbol is AAPL, and Tesla's is
TSLA (Figure 6). Some stocks are part of an index that is used to
judge how the overall stock market is performing. You may have
heard of the Dow Jones Industrial Average (DJIA – Figure 7) or

the Dow as it is typically called, the NASDAQ or the S&P 500. Each index has specific criteria to determine the stocks it includes. Which way each index is heading, either up or down, can be an indication of how healthy the economy or a particular segment of it is.

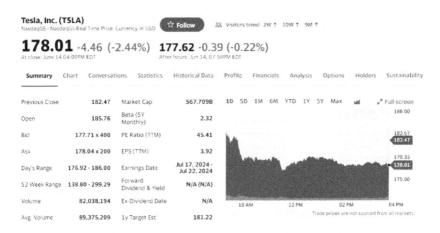

Figure 6 - Tesla Stock on Yahoo Finance

Figure 7 - DJIA chart from Google Finance

Many people find owning stocks appealing because they offer the potential for significant financial growth. Stocks are highly liquid, meaning they are easy to buy and sell. While most investors buy stocks for their appreciation, some also look for stocks that pay dividends. A dividend is a portion of the company's profit paid back to the owners, usually every quarter. Insurance companies and utility companies are good sources of dividends, although any company may pay one.

When you receive a dividend, you have several options. You can choose to spend it, invest it elsewhere, or, if the company offers it, reinvest it in more shares through their dividend reinvestment plan. This plan is a great way to automate your investments. While the dividend may seem small at first, over time, it can accumulate to a significant amount, especially if the stock's value also increases. It's important to remember that regardless of how you use the dividend, it's considered income and should be reported on your tax return.

Among the various investment options, stocks are considered to be among the riskiest. The price of a stock is influenced by numerous factors, many of which are beyond your control. Changes in management, government policies, supply chain issues, global events, and even public opinion can significantly impact a stock's value. This is why it's crucial to conduct thorough research before investing in stocks and to monitor them regularly. Active involvement in your investments can foster a sense of responsibility and engagement.

Preferred stock combines features of both stocks and bonds. Since it is a stock, investors are owners. However, they don't have voting rights. And similar to bonds, they pay a fixed dividend. Prices are generally more stable, too. Preferred stocks can either be perpetual or callable, meaning the company can retire them at some point, just like a bond. Investors are drawn to them because the dividends are more consistent than common stock dividends and higher than bond payments. This stability can provide a sense of security and confidence in your investment choice.

Bonds

Buying a bond means that you are loaning money to a company or the government, and they pay you back with interest. In essence, you are the bank. As a creditor, if the company were to go out of business, you would be paid back ahead of stockholders. This provides a layer of protection for investors. When a bond is issued by a company, it is called a corporate bond. When it's issued by the federal government, it is a treasury bill, note, or bond, depending on when it matures. And bonds issued by other government bodies are called municipal bonds.

The easiest way to explain how they work is to give you an example. Let's say you buy a $1000 3-year U.S. Treasury note that is paying 4% annual interest (the coupon rate) from TreasuryDirect.gov. Every six months, you'll receive $20 in interest. We compute that by multiplying $1000 x .04 to get $40 for the annual interest, then dividing that by two payments per year. At the end of the third year, you'll get your last $20 interest payment plus your original $1000. Corporate and municipal bonds work the same way, though they may pay quarterly or annually.

Most bonds are set up like this. However, there is another type of bond called a "no coupon" bond. They work a little differently. Instead of paying face value for the bond and receiving interest payments, you buy the bond at a discount and cash it in at maturity for face value. An example of this is a U.S. Savings bond. If you purchased a savings bond today with a face value of $100, it would cost you about $27.00. You could cash it in any time after the first year, but you would only get your original $27 plus annual interest of 2.7% (the rate for 2024). In order to receive the face value amount, you'll have to wait 20 years.

To simplify things from here on out, we'll refer to corporate and municipal bonds as "bonds" and U.S. Treasury bills, notes, and bonds as "treasuries." Although stocks and bonds are different investments, they are alike in several ways. Just like stocks, bonds have a ticker symbol, raise capital through IPOs, are traded on their own market, and are purchased through the same brokers. They are also just as liquid. The same things that cause a stock price to rise or fall can also affect bond and treasury prices. Unlike stocks and bonds, though, treasuries are also directly influenced by the federal funds rate set by the Federal Reserve.

ISSUE	MATURITY DATE	COUPON	YIELD
US50077LAB27	6/1/2046	4.375%	5.8078%
US50077LAV80	4/1/2030	3.750%	5.0953%
US50077LAT34	1/30/2029	4.625%	4.9752%
US423074AF08	7/15/2028	6.375%	5.2126%

Figure 8 – Kraft Corporation Bond Listings

Figure 8 shows a list of Kraft's outstanding bonds. The maturity date is the day the company retires the debt and returns the face value of the bond to the investor. The coupon rate is the interest rate at which the bond was issued. The yield is the interest rate you would receive if you bought the bond today on the open market. It differs from the coupon rate when the price of the bond is higher or lower than its face value. In short, bonds and treasuries can trade at three different levels:

- At a premium – the price is higher than the face value, and your yield is lower.
- At par – the price is equal to face value, making the yield equal to the coupon rate.
- At a discount – the price is lower than the face value, and your yield is higher.

Let's see how that would affect our T-note investment from above. Remember, we bought a $1000 T-note at 4% interest, equal to $40 per year. If the note is trading at a premium of $1050, we still only receive $40 of interest, which lowers our yield to 3.8% ($40 / $1050 = .038). If we are lucky enough to buy it at a discount of $950, our yield will go up to 4.21% ($40 / $950 = .0421).

Every bond has a rating between AAA and C, which acts as the company's credit score. Typically speaking, the higher the rating, the lower the interest rate investors are willing to accept. AAA bonds are the safest investments, but anything BBB and better is considered investment grade. Bonds with lower credit ratings pay considerably higher interest rates. These high-yield or "junk" bonds are usually pretty risky.

Mutual Funds, ETFs, and REITs

If you'd like to own paper assets, commodities, or real estate but don't want to research individual companies, mutual funds, ETFs (Exchange-Traded Funds), and REITs (Real Estate Investment Trusts) may be a good fit for you. While they are all popular investment vehicles, they serve different purposes and operate in distinct ways.

A mutual fund pools money from many investors to buy a diversified portfolio of stocks, bonds, or other securities. It is managed by a professional fund manager who makes investment decisions on behalf of the fund's investors. They became popular in the 1980s when companies moved from offering pensions to 401k accounts to their employees. In fact, they are the predominant option in many 401ks. Vanguard, Blackrock, and Fidelity are three companies that consistently have top-performing funds.

Shares of mutual funds are bought and sold at the end of the trading day based on their net asset value (NAV), which is calculated by adding up the value of all the component investments and dividing it by the number of mutual fund shares. Their investment Focus can be broadly diversified or focused on specific sectors like high tech or healthcare, regions like South America or emerging markets, or investment strategies.

Like mutual funds, ETFs pool investor money to invest in portfolios of assets, but they trade on stock exchanges in a way that is similar to individual stocks. They are traded throughout the trading day at market prices that can fluctuate continuously, often making them more liquid and price-transparent than mutual funds. ETFs can track indexes, specific sectors, and commodities or employ various investment strategies, including those used by mutual funds. Examples of top-performing funds in 2024 are The Invesco QQQ Trust Series I (ticker symbol QQQ), which invests in stocks across many different sectors, and the SPDR Gold Shares fund (ticker symbol GLD), which invests in gold bullion.

REITs are companies that own or finance income-producing real estate across a range of property sectors. Investors buy shares in the REIT, effectively becoming partial owners of its real estate assets. REITs are traded on major exchanges like stocks, offering daily liquidity, though less frequently with some specialized or smaller REITs. While mutual funds and EFTs invest in many different assets, REITs specifically focus on real estate, which can include residential, commercial, and industrial properties. They are required to pay out at least 90% of their taxable income as dividends to shareholders.

Let's summarize these three fund types' more important differences:

- **Liquidity**: ETFs generally offer the highest liquidity, followed by REITs and mutual funds.
- **Management**: Mutual funds are actively managed more often, whereas ETFs are typically passively managed, tracking an index. REITs are managed by a trust that maintains and manages the property holdings.
- **Income Generation**: REITs are particularly noted for potentially high dividend yields, reflecting their requirement to distribute most of their income. Mutual funds and ETFs may also pay dividends, depending on the underlying assets.
- **Investment Objective**: While mutual funds and ETFs can vary greatly in their objectives (growth, value, income, etc.), REITs specifically aim to generate income through real estate investments, offering a way to invest in real estate without directly owning property.

Investment	Mutual Fund	ETF	REIT
Assets	Stocks, Bonds, Money Markets	Stocks, Bonds, Commodities, Currencies	Real Estate
Where to Buy	Broker, Issuing Company	Broker	Broker
Main Objective	Appreciation	Appreciation	Income

Figure 9 – Investment Fund Comparison

Despite their advantages, all of these funds have drawbacks you need to consider, too. Investors in mutual funds, ETFs, and REITs can expect to be charged several types of fees. Management fees are standard across all these investments, compensating fund managers or trusts for their expertise in managing the portfolio. Transaction fees also apply, particularly when buying or selling assets within the fund or trust, and these can vary depending on the frequency and type of transactions involved.

Additionally, some investments may have load fees (specific to mutual funds) that are charged at the time of purchase or sale of shares. For those trading ETFs, brokerage commissions and bid-ask spreads are important to consider, as these affect the cost of trading shares on the open market. Lastly, operational fees cover the administrative and operational costs associated with managing the investments.

Fees aren't necessarily bad, but you have to remember to subtract them from your expected return when you're evaluating different investment options. For example, if you think the fund will earn you 10% on your investment, but they charge 4% each year you own it, your actual return is only 6%.

Lastly, you need to be aware of the taxes on dividends. When stocks owned by your fund pay out dividends, they aren't paid out in cash to you but are put right back into the fund. However, you still have to pay taxes on them. It's like being taxed on money you've earned but haven't seen yet. It's good to keep this in mind because it affects how much you actually make from your investments, especially when tax time rolls around.

Peer-to-Peer Lending

If the thought of being the bank sounded fun when we went over bonds, you'll really like this. Peer-to-peer lending sites bring together people who need a loan for any number of reasons with people who are willing to lend them money. If you're familiar with Kickstarter or GoFundMe, then you know how it works. In case you're not, we'll look at an example.

A couple wants to borrow $5000 to upgrade their kitchen, so they apply on a site like Prosper.com for a loan. Prosper evaluates their situation and gives them a rating from A.A. to E. Just like with bonds, the higher the rating, the lower the borrower's interest rate. Next, Prosper lists the loan information, including the interest rate, for investors to consider.

This is where you come in. After evaluating the borrower's loan profile (you can't see any personal information), you decide you'd like to own the loan. You have $1000 to invest, but you're concerned about putting it all in one place. Fortunately, it's possible to fund just a small portion for as little as $25. Over the next few days, other investors contribute, too, until the entire amount is funded. At that point, the couple gets their loan, and you receive a monthly payment.

You might be thinking that there is no way you can get rich by owning one $25 loan, and you're right. But if you invest consistently, over time, you can build up hundreds or even thousands of dollars of passive monthly income.

Real Assets

Most financial advisors will say you need a diversified portfolio. By that, they mean you need to own a mix of paper assets. However, to be truly diversified, you should also invest in some tangible assets like real estate, precious metals, or collectibles. Regardless of what the experts say, the best portfolio is one in which you feel comfortable investing. You'll potentially be investing for decades, so it's wise to choose investments that will hold your interest. You may not enjoy the ups and downs of the stock market, so it's important to know there are other options for investing your money. Let's look at some of them.

Real Estate

There are almost as many ways to invest in real estate as there are properties. And the list of benefits is long, too. I'll list a few of them.

- One investment can potentially generate both income and appreciation.
- You have much more control over the investment than with paper assets.
- You help raise the value of the whole community when you take care of your properties.
- It's harder to lose ALL of your money. Even if a house burns down, the land still has value, and hopefully, you have insurance!

- It enables you to use your creativity and handyman skills if that's your thing.
- You can be an active or passive investor and make money either way.

Maybe you're a fan of the home renovation shows on HGTV where the owner fixes up a house and then "flips" it for a profit. Flipping houses is one example of active investing, which is when an investor is involved in the day-to-day activities of the company. Managing a rental property yourself is another active investing activity. One of the benefits of being an active investor is the tax advantages. It's too complicated to go into here, but suffice it to say that active investors are able to take deductions on their tax returns that passive investors cannot.

On the flip side, you can do just as well as a passive investor. If you like real estate but don't want to actively manage a business, this might be the option for you. It doesn't mean, however, that you don't have to know anything about real estate – you should still be able to analyze a deal yourself or with the help of an accountant.

Besides REITs that were discussed earlier, you can passively invest in real estate through several different crowd-funding sites, like CrowdStreet.com, that function just like the peer-to-peer lending example above. The difference is instead of individuals looking for loans, it's one real estate investing company that owns all the properties. This may sound like it's the same thing as a REIT, but it's not. With a REIT, you own shares of the fund that owns the properties. With a crowd-funded investment, you are a general partner in the company that owns the properties.

It's a small distinction but an important one that comes into play when we look at who is eligible to invest in them. Since REITs are publicly traded on an exchange, they are monitored by the Securities and Exchange Commission or SEC, just like other paper assets. This level of scrutiny is in place so that anyone can invest in them, knowing they have been vetted and are legitimate investments.

Real estate companies that offer crowd-funded opportunities are not publicly traded and, therefore, aren't required to comply with all of the same regulations. Instead, these investments are only open to savvier, "accredited" investors with a net worth of $1 million or more or income of $200,000 per year for at least two years. As a teen, it's probably safe to say you're not at that level yet, but it's something to shoot for!

Collectibles

Almost anything can be a collectible, but not all collectibles are suitable for long-term investments. That doesn't mean you can't make money collecting action figures or Air Jordans. Though, for investment purposes, we're talking about items that historically have appreciated in value decade after decade.

Investing in art can be an exciting and rewarding way to diversify your portfolio, especially for young investors looking to explore non-traditional assets. Art investing involves buying pieces of fine art—like paintings, sculptures, or photographs—in hopes that their value will increase over time. This type of investment is unique because it allows you to own tangible, aesthetic items that can be displayed and enjoyed, not just held as digital or paper assets.

However, art investing does require a keen eye and some expertise. The value of art can be highly subjective, influenced by factors such as the artist's reputation, the rarity of the work, and current trends in the art world. It's often recommended for beginners to start by attending art exhibitions, following art auctions, and perhaps consulting with art advisors to gain knowledge and insights into the art market.

While art can provide substantial returns, it's also important to note that it can be illiquid, meaning it might take time to sell an artwork for a fair price. Therefore, art should be viewed as a long-term investment, and it's wise to balance it with more liquid assets in a diversified investment portfolio.

Precious Metals

Investing in precious metals like gold, silver, platinum, and palladium is a classic strategy for diversifying an investment portfolio and protecting against inflation. Precious metals are considered a "safe haven" during times of economic uncertainty because they typically hold their value or even appreciate when other investments might be declining.

Precious metals can be an accessible entry point into the world of investing for young investors. They can be purchased in various forms, including physical bars, coins, and investment-grade jewelry, online or at your local coin shop.

It's important to understand that while precious metals can provide stability, they do not yield dividends or interest like stocks or bonds. Therefore, they should be part of a broader, well-rounded investment strategy. Additionally, prices for metals can be volatile in the short term, driven by global economic factors. Hence, investors need to be prepared for potential fluctuations in their investment value.

FinLit Fast Track

Activities

1. If you didn't include an amount for investing in your budget in chapter 6, add it now. If you have to allocate a bit of your savings for it, that's ok. As your income grows, you can bump your savings rate back up.
2. Choose the investment that you're most interested in and research it more thoroughly. Determine if there is a way you can invest now with the money you have available or if you'll have to save up before you can jump in.
3. Take this short quiz to determine your risk tolerance: https://FinLitFastTrack.com/risk
4. Visit a local coin store and purchase a silver dollar or two. Ask the salesclerk to explain the difference between the spot price and the purchase price.

Dummy Trading Portfolio

Let's have some fun with investing without the possibility of losing money! There are lots of sites where you can create a dummy trading portfolio to gain an understanding of how trading works. Why not challenge your friends to set one up as well and see who can get the highest profits in your hypothetical portfolios? It's a ton of fun, and whoever wins can share some of their secrets or guidelines on how they got their portfolio to grow so much.

Some of the sites you can try are Wall Street Survivor, MarketWatch Virtual Stock Exchange, and Mockportfolios.com.

Questions

1. What assets or investment classes are you considering for creating a diversified portfolio?
2. What is your plan for ongoing investment education and staying informed about your investment portfolio?
3. How do you plan to track and monitor the performance of your investments over time?
4. Have you discussed your investment goals and strategies with peers, family members, or friends, and what insights or questions emerged from these conversations?
5. What will your strategy be to stay disciplined and avoid emotional decisions in response to market fluctuations or news events that may impact your investments?

In this chapter, you ventured into the dynamic world of investing, unlocking the potential for financial growth. You learned about the delicate balance between risk and reward, the importance of diversification, and the various types of investments available to you.

In the upcoming chapter, we'll explore the realm of insurance, a critical component of financial planning. You'll discover the importance of protecting your financial well-being and assets, understand the various types of insurance policies, and learn how insurance can provide you with peace of mind.

CHAPTER 9
YOUR SAFETY NET

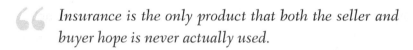 *Insurance is the only product that both the seller and buyer hope is never actually used.*

UNKNOWN

Many people don't realize how important insurance is because they have never been taught about it. Sometimes, when money gets tight, one of the first things adults do is cancel their insurance. But actually, that should be the last thing you do! Think of insurance as your safety net. If something goes wrong, it's there to catch you, so it's not something you'd want to get rid of.

Insurance is basically there for the "just in case" situations. A lot of people take the risk and go without it, hoping nothing bad will happen instead of having insurance to back them up if it does. Insurance is like a promise that you'll be taken care of if something unexpected happens. Keeping insurance can save you a ton of money in the long run because what you pay for insurance is usually much less than what you'd have to pay out of pocket for emergencies.

TYPES OF INSURANCE

You should be familiar with a few different types of insurance, but we will specifically look at auto and renter's insurance. There are many other types as well, including business, health, pet, home, life, travel, etc.

Auto Insurance

Auto insurance, often known as car insurance, empowers you with financial protection for your vehicle in various situations, such as accidents, theft, or damage from natural disasters. The extent of coverage is determined by the type of insurance policy you choose. Understanding the different types of coverage available is not just crucial, but it also gives you the confidence to make informed decisions. While adding more features can increase the cost of your insurance, investing in comprehensive coverage is generally a smart move. Here are the primary coverages to consider.

1. Liability insurance: This is required by law in most states. If an accident is your fault, bodily liability coverage will cover any injuries to the other people involved in the accident, like the other drivers and their passengers, as well as legal costs if they decide to sue you. You can also get property damage liability, which will pay for damages to property, like the other cars involved.
2. Collision insurance: If you finance your car, you're required to have collision coverage. This ensures that if

you're involved in any collision—whether with another vehicle or an object—damages to your car will be covered.

3. Comprehensive insurance: This coverage is also mandatory if your car is financed. It covers damage to your vehicle not caused by a collision, such as theft, vandalism, a falling tree, etc.

4. Medical payments: This type of insurance covers medical bills for you and all passengers in your car, regardless of who is at fault for the accident. It is mandatory in some states.

5. Personal injury protection: This is similar to medical payments but covers all medical expenses, including lost wages, rehabilitation costs, and funeral expenses. It is also required in some states.

6. Uninsured / Uninsured motorist insurance: This insurance is mandatory in some states and provides coverage for medical expenses and lost wages for you and all passengers in your vehicle if the other driver is uninsured or underinsured. Additionally, a component known as uninsured motorist property damage covers any damage to your car caused by an uninsured driver. Some states require both types of coverage.

Besides these, several optional coverages, such as towing, roadside assistance, and rental car reimbursement, may be useful.

Your car insurance premium depends on several factors, including the add-ons and your age. It can become quite pricey, but there are a few ways to save on it.

1. Choose a practical car: By choosing a small but reliable car, you can pay much less on insurance than someone who drives a fast or expensive car.

2. Consider a defensive driving course: Some insurances will lower your premium if you have completed an accident prevention or defensive driving course.

3. Find ways to improve your credit rating: Most insurers check your credit report when determining your premium. In the next chapter, we will examine your credit rating and how to improve it.

4. Good grades count: Many insurance companies offer a discount for maintaining a "B" average or better in high school or college.

5. Increase the deductibles: A deductible is the amount of money you have to pay before the insurance coverage kicks in. The higher your deductible, the lower your monthly premium will be. However, be cautious not to set a deductible higher than what you have in savings.

6. Make use of mass transit: Consider using your car less often if possible. Some insurers offer lower rates for drivers who log fewer miles, typically under a threshold of 7,500 miles per year.

7. Weigh up your options: There are quite a few different insurers to choose from. Get a quote from more than one and choose the best option. Remember to compare like for like, i.e., compare premiums where the level of coverage is the same.

Renter's Insurance

You don't have to worry about this if you are still living with your parents, but you will need to look at it once you move into your first place. Having this insurance protects you as the tenant from certain unforeseeable events. If something should happen, it will cover the damages, so you don't have to.

Although not required by law in all states, renter's insurance is essential for teens because:

- Your lease agreement might require it. Even if the law doesn't require you to have it, your landlord is allowed to include it as a clause in your lease agreement.
- Your personal belongings are covered. Your landlord's insurance will cover any damage to the structure; however, if you don't have renter's insurance, your personal belongings are at risk.
- It covers your visitors. If someone visits you and is injured, the personal liability coverage on your renter's insurance will cover their expenses.
- You always have a plan B. Suppose something happens that makes your apartment unlivable. In that case, renter's insurance may cover lodging and food expenses while your home is being repaired.

Renter's insurance is quite affordable, but there are a few things that can affect your premium. Just like with car insurance, there are specific ways you can save on your renter's insurance.

1. **Coverage limits:** The more the insurance covers, the more you will pay. Ideally, you want to have enough coverage to replace everything in the case of a complete loss. Still, if you don't have the budget for it, then you can take out a smaller policy and cover the essentials. Keep in mind, too, that com-

puters and other high-ticket items may require   special-ized coverage.

2. **Deductible value:** Choosing a higher deductible can reduce your premium. However, keep in mind that you'll need to pay this deductible out of pocket before your insurance coverage kicks in. This is one of the key reasons for maintaining an emergency fund.

3. **Bundling:** Most insurers offer a multiple-policy discount if you also insure your car with them.

4. **Safety features:** The safer your personal belongings are, the cheaper your premium could be. If you have safety locks and an alarm system, you might pay less on your premium than someone who doesn't.

5. **Type of coverage:** There are two main types of renters insurance:

   a. Actual cash value: Insuring at the actual cost allows the insurer to pay out whatever the current market value is for the item. This might not be enough to replace all of your belongings.

   b. Replacement cost: Choosing this type of insurance means that the insurer will pay out the amount to replace everything.

6. **Your location:** Where you live can also have an impact on your premium. In high-crime areas, the premium will be higher because there is a bigger chance that you will be a victim of theft. Similarly, your premium will increase if your area is prone to natural disasters.

7. **Compare quotes:** Just as with auto insurance, renter's insurance can vary from company to company. Get several quotes before making a decision.

Extended Warranties

Extended warranties are insurance you can buy to help cover the cost of repairs or replacements for electronics, appliances, and cars after the regular warranty runs out. When you buy something expensive, like a laptop or a fridge, you might be offered an extended warranty at the checkout. This means if something goes wrong with your item after the usual warranty period, the extended warranty will fix or replace it for a small or no deductible.

Whether you should get one depends on a few things: the cost of the item, how likely it is to break, how much repairs usually cost, and how much money you have in your emergency fund. For cheaper items, paying extra for an extended warranty might not make sense because it could cost more than just replacing the item. But for really pricey things, like a car or a high-end phone, where repairs are expensive, the extra cost of an extended warranty might be worth it for the peace of mind it gives you. Personally, I have purchased extended warranties on many products. Sometimes, it seemed like a waste of money, but other times, I was thankful that I had it.

Before you say yes to an extended warranty, make sure you understand what it covers and what it doesn't. Sometimes, the coverage you already have from the manufacturer's warranty is enough, or the product might be reliable enough not to need extra coverage. So, it's all about weighing the cost against the potential benefits.

FinLit Fast Track

Activities

1. Get the insurance policy declarations page for your or your parent's car. If neither of you have it, call your agent to get a copy or go online and download it. Review all of the different coverages, their limits, and how much each one costs. Check to see what discounts you receive. Ask you agent if there are any others you might qualify for.

2. Make an inventory of your belongings. You may be surprised at how much money you have invested in your stuff. Write down two values for each item – the original price and what it would cost to replace it. It's okay to make a lump sum estimate for clothes and such. Start keeping receipts for long-lasting items that cost more than $100, like your phone. If you do ever have an insurance claim, you'll need them to prove your item's value.

Questions

1. Can you explain the difference between actual cash value and replacement cost?

2. What products have you owned where an extended warranty would have been useful?

You have learned about insurance, types of insurance, and the benefits of taking advantage of the safety net. In Part V, we explore the concept of borrowing, debt, credit scores, and financial responsibility (renting your first apartment and big-ticket purchases).

The next chapter explores the realms of borrowing and debt, along with the crucial concept of credit scores. You'll gain insights into responsible borrowing, managing debt, and the impact of credit scores on your financial life.

PART FIVE

PART FIVE

CHAPTER 10
BE A CREDIT WISE TEEN

66 *Nothing changes your life more, other than God and love, than moving your credit score 120 points!*

JOHN HOPE BRYANT, CEO OF OPERATION HOPE

U nderstanding your credit score is crucial as it significantly impacts various aspects of your life. It can influence insurance premiums, borrowing rates, and even your eligibility for car or home loans. The decisions you make today can have long-term consequences, so it's essential to grasp the importance of your credit score.

Any credit or loans you apply for, and defaults on any payments (including insurance premiums) influence your credit score. We'll take a deeper dive into credit score, what it is, and how it's influenced later in this chapter.

THE GOOD AND THE BAD OF DEBT

Debt can be advantageous when it allows you to make investments in your future. For example, taking out student loans can pay off by helping you get a degree that leads to a well-paying job. Similarly, a mortgage can help you buy a home, which might increase in value over time. Sometimes, debt is necessary for starting a business or buying a car needed for commuting. Used strategically, debt can help build your credit score. By consistently making on-time payments, you demonstrate to future lenders that you're a responsible borrower, which can make it easier and cheaper to borrow money in the future.

However, debt comes with risks and costs. The most obvious is the interest you have to pay on top of what you borrowed. This can add up, especially with high-interest debt like credit cards, making it harder to pay off what you owe. If not managed properly, debt can spiral out of control, leading to a low credit score, which makes borrowing more expensive or even impossible in the future. Excessive debt can also limit your financial freedom, tying up your future income and putting you in a position where a financial emergency could lead to severe consequences like bankruptcy.

BORROWING BASICS

Borrowing money is a fundamental financial tool that can help you manage your expenses, invest in opportunities, or cover unexpected emergencies. Typically, there are two main ways to borrow money: taking out a loan or using credit. Each method serves different needs and comes with its own set of rules and considerations.

When you take out a loan, you receive a specific amount of money from a lender, which you agree to pay back over a set period, usually with interest. Loans are often used for substantial one-time expenses, such as buying a car, paying for college, or purchasing a home. They can be categorized into various types, including personal loans, student loans, mortgages, and auto loans, each designed to fit specific financing needs.

On the other hand, using credit involves borrowing money up to a specific limit whenever you need it and paying it back over time. Credit cards are the most common form of this type of borrowing. They give you ongoing access to funds as long as you stay within your credit limit. Credit can be incredibly flexible, allowing you to manage cash flow for daily expenses, take advantage of rewards programs, or handle emergencies. However, discipline is required to manage them effectively and avoid high-interest charges and debt accumulation.

Understanding the ins and outs of borrowing methods empowers you to make informed financial decisions. This knowledge can help you choose the right option for your current needs and future goals, putting you in control of your financial journey.

Loans

Taking out a loan might seem like a good solution when you urgently need money. Even so, it's important to make a thoughtful, informed decision. A loan involves borrowing a specific amount of money, typically for a designated purpose, which you then repay over time with monthly payments. The total amount you pay back will include the original sum borrowed plus interest.

Before we get into the types of loans, there are some important terms we need to cover.

- Fixed-rate loans are loans where the interest rate is fixed for the duration of the loan.
- Variable-rate loans are the opposite of fixed-rate loans. The interest rate will change with the prime rate and can change monthly, quarterly, or annually.
- A term loan lets you pay back a loan in equal installments over a set period. Car loans and home loans fall in this category.
- A secured loan is a loan where the lender has collateral they can take or keep if you miss any payments. An auto loan is a secured loan.
- An unsecured or signature loan is where the lender gives you the money with no collateral. Vacation or Christmas loans offered by local banks are examples of these.
- APR stands for annual percentage rate. This is the actual rate of the loan when all of the fees, not just the interest, are accounted for.

These days, you can get a loan for almost anything. The most common types include auto loans, home loans, personal loans, student loans, business loans, and debt consolidation loans. One type of loan to steer clear of, though, is the payday loan. These loans might seem harmless at first because they don't charge traditional interest but instead include a finance charge. But don't be fooled; they are the most expensive credit you can get.

Let me give you an example. If you borrow $200 with a 15% finance charge, you'll need to pay back $230 in no more than two weeks. While a $30 charge might not seem too daunting, if this rate is annualized, it translates to an astonishing 390% APR! Is there any wonder why there's a location on every block? We arrive at this number by dividing 52 weeks by the two-week loan period and multiplying that by the finance charge (52 weeks / 2 weeks * 15%).

Before you decide to take out any loan, it's crucial to evaluate all associated costs, not just the initial amount borrowed. Lenders often charge additional fees, such as processing fees, which might be deducted from the loan amount. Some loans also come with a prepayment penalty if you pay them off early. Always request a detailed breakdown of all costs, including total interest for the duration of the loan, especially if it's a fixed-rate loan.

Just like insurers, lenders can also have different interest rates. When you're looking for a loan, make sure to shop around and keep these tips in mind:

- Be organized: Whatever you receive during the loan application period or have to provide, keep copies of it in a folder so that it's easy to find again. It can be physical or digital.
- Understand all the details of your loan: Before you accept the terms of your loan, make sure that you understand all of the terms. If something is unclear, ask for clarity so that you're not caught unaware of any hidden costs. And read the fine print!
- Only borrow what you need: If you only need $100, don't borrow $200, even if the lender offers you more. The more you borrow, the more interest you will pay in the long run.
- Check your credit score first: A lender is more likely to give you a loan and reduce your interest rate if you have a

good credit score. Before applying for a loan, check what your credit score is and try to improve it.

Finally, it's vital to consider your ability to repay the loan. Even if you're in a pinch for cash, taking on a loan that you cannot afford to repay can lead to a distressing cycle of debt. Continually assess your financial situation to ensure you can meet the repayment terms without needing to borrow more money.

Credit Cards

Obtaining a credit card can be an effective way to build and enhance your credit score. While some believe that credit cards are inherently risky, they can be beneficial when used responsibly. It's essential to remember that responsible use of a credit card is almost mandatory to achieve a high credit score.

When considering your first credit card, it's essential to know what to expect and how to choose the correct option, especially if you're just starting to build your credit history. Most credit card companies require applicants to have some credit history and a source of income to show that they're able to repay any money they borrow. However, if you're a teen, you might not have enough credit history to get approved for a standard credit card.

That's where a secured credit card comes into play. A secured credit card is a fantastic starter option for those with no credit or low credit scores. Unlike typical credit cards, a secured card requires you to make a cash deposit upfront. This deposit usually sets your credit limit. For example, if you deposit $300, your credit limit will likely be $300. This deposit is used as security by the credit card company, which means they can use it to cover any payments if you fail to make them.

Using a secured credit card responsibly can help you build or rebuild your credit. Each time you make a purchase and then pay it off by the due date, the credit card company reports this good behavior to the credit bureaus. Over time, your credit score can improve, making you eligible for regular credit cards with better benefits, like lower interest rates and reward programs. Just make sure to always spend within your means and pay your balance in full each month to avoid interest charges and build a positive credit history.

Now, I want to caution you about store credit cards. You've likely been prompted at checkout to open one for a significant discount on your purchase. Although they're easy to obtain, they generally offer little benefit to your credit report. They can be detrimental if not managed wisely. It's okay to have one or two for your favorite stores, but having several can make you appear risky to credit bureaus.

Maintaining self-control when using credit cards is crucial. It's easy to fall into credit card traps by making impulsive purchases beyond your means. Such behavior can quickly lead to mounting balances, increased minimum payments, and steep interest rates. If the debt becomes overwhelming, it can severely damage your credit score and make it difficult to manage your financial obligations. In extreme cases, if you can't keep up with payments, creditors may freeze your card. It's important to note that they could even take legal action, which underscores the seriousness of the situation and the need for immediate action.

If you find yourself in too much credit card debt, escaping can be challenging, but it's possible. First, stop using your card. Then, consider these steps:

1. Increase your payments by reducing expenses elsewhere in your budget. Consider starting a side hustle if needed.
2. Contact your credit card company to inquire if they can reduce your interest rate, especially if you've maintained a good payment history.
3. If you're behind on payments, reach out to a credit counseling service. They can negotiate on your behalf to lower your owed amount and establish a manageable repayment plan. However, be aware that this could lead to your account being closed and a significant drop in your credit score.
4. Bankruptcy should be a last resort, as it impacts your credit report for 7-10 years, during which time securing new credit becomes more difficult and expensive.

To avoid falling into the debt trap, adopt these proactive strategies: First, set up reminders for your payment due dates to ensure you never miss a deadline. It's best to pay your bills before the due date; the earlier, the better. Your goal should be to pay off the entire balance every month, but if that isn't an option, always pay more than the minimum due. Average interest rates across the industry are above 27% (Black, 2024), making it very easy to fall behind. Lastly, consider enabling autopay on your online banking platform or app, which can help you stay consistent with your payments and avoid any late fees.

CREDIT SCORE

Your credit score is a three-digit number that reflects your credit-worthiness, ranging from 300 to 850. A higher score indicates greater creditworthiness. This score is determined by several factors:

- Your payment history.
- The total amount of debt you currently owe.
- The length of your credit history.
- The types of credit accounts you hold.
- Any new credit accounts you've recently opened.

A score of 700 or above is considered very good and can qualify you for the best loan rates. If your score is significantly lower, don't worry—it takes time to build a robust credit history.

In the United States, credit scores are primarily tracked by three major credit reporting agencies—TransUnion, Equifax, and Experian—along with several smaller agencies. These agencies receive monthly updates from your creditors and compile this information into a credit report, which is accessible to both you and potential lenders. Your score is calculated using formulas developed by the Fair Isaac Corporation, or FICO. Each credit bureau uses a slightly different formula, which is why your score may vary between them.

While FICO keeps its scoring formulas confidential, it does disclose the key factors considered in scoring, which are summarized in Figure 10. Most of these factors are straightforward, but terms like 'new credit' and 'credit mix' may need some explanation. 'New credit' refers to the number of accounts you've opened in the past year; opening one or two is fine, but more could lower your score. 'Credit mix' refers to the variety of credit types you manage, such as installment loans (like auto or home loans), major credit cards, and retail cards.

Figure 10 – FICO score criteria breakdown

Be cautious of websites offering free credit scores; many of these do not provide a FICO score, which is the standard used by most lenders for credit decisions. These alternative scores may not be helpful in predicting how lenders will view your creditworthiness.

Maintaining a good credit score is crucial, as it can secure you lower interest rates on loans and make you more attractive to lenders, potentially eliminating the need for a cosigner. A cosigner is someone who agrees to take responsibility for your loan if you fail to meet your obligations.

Here's how you can build a good credit score, which your future self will thank you for:

- Ask your parents whether you can be an authorized user on their account. This means that their account history will become part of your credit report. If they have a good credit score, you will benefit from it.

- Don't max out your card: Whether it's a major credit card or a store card, don't use too much credit. The rule of thumb is to limit your balance to at most 25% of your available credit.
- Always pay on time: This applies to whatever you need to pay. Never miss a payment or be late.
- Check your credit report annually to see what you can do to improve: You can download your report for free from AnnualCreditReport.com and receive tips on how to improve your score. The report will also show you what affected your credit score the most. MyFico.com also makes credit scores available for free.
- Be patient: Rome wasn't built in a day, as they say, and neither is a solid credit report. Although there are many things you can do to increase your score, having a long credit history takes time.

FinLit Fast Track

Activities

1. As a teen, you may or may not have a credit record. To find out if you do, go to AnnualCreditreport.com and try ordering one or all three reports. If you do have a report, next go to MyFico.com and sign up for the free credit score monitoring.
2. If you have a credit card, check your statement for the interest rate. Is it a fixed rate or variable?
3. Start building your credit with the help of your parents using this strategy.

a. Go to a local bank or credit union and get a 12-month secured loan for a small amount - $500 to $1000. Your parent will probably have to cosign.

b. Make sure you can afford the monthly payment.

c. Put that loan proceeds in a savings account as collateral, and make sure the bank will release the funds as the loan is paid down.

d. After you make six payments, withdraw enough money from the savings account to pay off the loan.

e. You now have a positive loan on your credit report that only cost you a little bit of interest.

f. Repeat with a larger amount if desired.

Questions

1. What is your plan for building your credit report?
2. If you have a credit card, what is your strategy for using it wisely?

In this chapter, you ventured into the crucial world of credit scores and debt, gaining valuable insights into financial responsibility.

In the upcoming chapter, we'll explore the realm of big-ticket purchases, focusing on significant financial decisions like buying a car and renting an apartment. You'll learn how to evaluate the true cost of car ownership, compute return on investment (ROI), and navigate the complexities of renting an apartment.

CHAPTER 11

YOUR FIRST APARTMENT AND BIG-TICKET PURCHASES

Some people want it to happen, some wish it would happen, others make it happen.

MICHAEL JORDAN, FORMER PRO
BASKETBALL PLAYER

Making significant financial decisions like buying your first car, going to college, or getting your first apartment are not just milestones, they are achievements. These moments are not just about learning how to handle financial responsibilities, they are about taking control of your future. As a teen, managing large expenses can seem daunting, but with the right approach, you can make these decisions confidently and wisely, feeling empowered by your ability to navigate these financial milestones.

Each of these purchases involves unique considerations. Buying a car not only requires upfront payment but also ongoing costs like insurance, maintenance, and fuel. College, on the other hand, is an investment in your future, demanding careful planning about how to cover tuition, books, and living expenses. Similarly, moving into your first apartment brings its own set of financial obligations, from rent and utilities to furnishing and possibly rental insurance.

This chapter will guide you through planning and executing these big-ticket purchases. You'll learn how to budget for large expenses, evaluate your financing options, and understand the long-term financial commitments involved. The skills you develop through this process will not only help you make informed decisions but also make you feel prepared and confident, ensuring that these significant steps are both exciting and sustainable for your financial future.

BUYING A CAR

Buying your first car is an exhilarating experience, offering a new sense of independence and the freedom to go wherever you want. However, it's easy to overlook the range of costs associated with owning a car, which can lead to unexpected stress instead of convenience. It's crucial to be aware of all the expenses involved to ensure that your vehicle doesn't become a financial burden.

Here's a list of typical expenses to consider when buying and owning a car:

- Purchase Price: The upfront cost of the car is the most obvious expense. Unless you're paying cash, you'll have a monthly loan payment for up to six years.
- Fuel Costs: All cars run on something, whether it's gasoline or electricity. Consider the current gas prices, your daily travel distance, and the car's fuel efficiency to calculate your monthly fuel expenses. If you prefer an

electric vehicle, remember to include the cost of charging it.

- Maintenance and Repairs: While both new and used cars come with warranties, they don't last forever. Used car warranties are especially short. Even with one, you'll still need to pay for:

    ○ Replacing tires
    ○ Changing brake pads
    ○ Replacing windshield wipers
    ○ Other miscellaneous repairs not covered by the warranty.

- Service Costs: If your car doesn't have a service plan, you'll need to pay for regular maintenance like oil changes every 6,000 to 12,000 miles or every 6 to 12 months.
- Insurance: Auto insurance is mandatory, whether your car is financed or not. The cost can vary based on the car model, your age, driving history, and coverage level. We covered car insurance in Chapter 9.
- Registration Fees and Taxes: You'll need to pay fees and taxes to register the car in your name. Rates vary widely from state to state and could run hundreds of dollars.
- Depreciation: Remember that a car's value decreases over time. The moment you drive your new vehicle off the lot, it starts to lose value, and you won't be able to sell it for the same amount you paid.

Before making a purchase, it's crucial to add up all these costs to see the true cost of owning a car. This will not only help you decide if you can really afford it without stretching your finances too thin but also make you feel informed and responsible. Understanding the full financial impact of owning a vehicle will prepare you better for this significant commitment, making you feel in control of your financial future.

Choosing a Car

Choosing your first car can be overwhelming with all the options available. How do you even start? Here are some straightforward tips to help you navigate the process of choosing and buying your first car.

1. Set a Budget: First, determine how much you can afford to spend. If you're paying in cash, you'll already know your limit. If you're considering vehicle financing, figure out how much you can manage for monthly payments. Remember, the cost of a car isn't just the price tag or the loan repayment; it includes fuel, insurance, maintenance, and other expenses we discussed earlier.

2. New vs. Secondhand: Decide whether you want a new car or a used one. New cars are more expensive upfront and for insurance, but they come with warranties and fewer initial maintenance issues. Secondhand cars can be great bargains, but they require more maintenance. If you opt for a secondhand car, always do your homework:

   a. Bring along someone knowledgeable about cars to check the vehicle.

   b. Ensure the car is in good condition and doesn't have significant issues that could become costly.

   c. Get a report of the car's damage history from Carfax.com.

3. Test Drive: Always test drive a car before you buy it. If you're considering several options, test drive each to see how they feel and perform. A car might look perfect but not feel right when you drive it. For secondhand vehicles, a test drive is crucial to check for any potential issues with how the car runs.

4. Negotiate: Once you've chosen a car, don't hesitate to negotiate the price. Car dealers often have wiggle room on price, especially since many work on commission.

By following these tips, you can make a more informed decision when buying your first car, ensuring you choose a vehicle that fits your budget and meets your needs without causing financial strain.

GOING TO COLLEGE

Deciding whether to go to college is a significant decision that can impact your life in many ways. While a college education can offer many benefits, it's essential to weigh these against the costs and consider all your options. Here's a closer look at the cost-benefit analysis of going to college to help you decide if it's the right choice for you.

What You Put In: The Cost of College

- Time: Earning a college degree takes about four years for a bachelor's degree, which is a substantial commitment. During this period, you would be focusing on studies, potentially limiting the time you can spend working full-time or pursuing other interests.

- Money: The financial cost of college is significant. Tuition fees can range from a few thousand dollars a year at public colleges to tens of thousands at private universities. On top of tuition, you need to consider the cost of books, supplies, housing, and other living expenses.

- Effort: College requires a considerable amount of effort and self-discipline. You'll need to attend classes, complete assignments, study for exams, and manage your time effectively. The academic rigor can be challenging, and the pressure to succeed can be intense.

What You Get in Return: Benefits of College

- Higher Income: Generally, one of the most compelling arguments for attending college is the potential for higher earnings. According to data from the Bureau of Labor Statistics, individuals with a bachelor's degree earn, on average, 65% more than those with just a high school diploma. Over a lifetime, this can significantly affect your financial stability and quality of life.

- Employment Opportunities: A college degree opens up a broader array of job opportunities that are often only available to those who have a degree. Many careers require a bachelor's as the minimum qualification.

- Networking Opportunities: College provides a unique environment to connect with peers, professors, and alums who can offer support and open doors to career opportunities. These networks can be invaluable as you enter the job market.

- Education: Beyond the career benefits, college offers the opportunity to gain extensive knowledge in your chosen field. This education can prepare you for specific careers and help you develop a well-rounded intellectual foundation.

- Personal Development: College isn't just about academic growth; it's also a crucial time for personal development. Students often experience significant growth in self-understanding, global awareness, and independence during their college years.

When College Might Not Be Worth It

- If a Degree Doesn't Lead to Professional Success: If your chosen career path doesn't require a college degree, investing in one might not offer a good return. For some trades and careers, vocational training or apprenticeships are more appropriate and cost-effective.
- If You Can't Afford It: Taking on substantial debt without a clear return on investment is risky. Suppose the cost of college is too burdensome. In that case, it might lead to long-term financial strain, especially if student loans are involved.
- If You Have Other Plans: College is a significant commitment, and if you have other things you want to pursue first or if you're unsure about what you want to do, it might be worth exploring those paths before committing to a degree.

If college is definitely in your future, there are a few things you can do to avoid taking out a loan or reduce the amount of the loan you need to apply for.

- Apply for scholarships or grants: If your grades are good or you're good at a particular sport, you may be considered for a scholarship or grant. These rarely require any repayments.
- Go to community college: Many states offer free community college. Those that are not free are a lot cheaper than four-year colleges. You can earn an associate degree at a community college and finish up a bachelor's degree at another college.
- Weigh up your options: Look at what each college or university charges for the degree you want and choose the most affordable one.
- Get a part-time job: Whether you are already starting college or still in school, look for a part-time job where you can earn an income that you can put toward your college fund.

While college can offer numerous benefits in terms of career options, earnings potential, and personal development, it's not the right path for everyone. Consider your career goals, financial situation, and personal circumstances carefully before deciding. Sometimes, gaining work experience, learning a trade, or even starting your own business might align better with your individual goals and financial realities.

RENTING AN APARTMENT

When you rent an apartment, you're agreeing to pay a landlord a fixed amount of money each month to live in a property. But the monthly rent isn't the only cost involved. There are several expenses you should be aware of when planning to rent your first place.

Typical Expenses When Renting an Apartment

1. Security Deposit: Most landlords require a security deposit before you move in. This deposit typically equals one month's rent but can vary depending on the landlord's policy and the state's regulations. The security deposit is held by the landlord as insurance against damage you might cause to the apartment or for unpaid rent. If you leave the apartment in good condition and all dues are clear, this deposit is refunded to you at the end of your lease.

2. First and Last Month's Rent: Many landlords also require tenants to pay the first and last month's rent upfront. This serves as a buffer for the landlord, ensuring they have funds in case you leave suddenly without paying or if repair needs arise after you move out.

3. Utilities: Depending on your lease agreement, you may be responsible for paying for utilities such as electricity, water, gas, internet, and cable. Some apartments include certain utilities in the rent, so you need to clarify what is included and what isn't. Each utility company may also require a deposit, especially if you don't have much credit.

4. Renter's Insurance: While not always mandatory, renter's insurance is highly recommended as it protects your belongings in case of theft, damage, or disasters. This insurance is generally affordable, costing about $15 to $30 per month, depending on the coverage amount. We covered it in more detail in chapter 9.

5. Application Fee and Credit Check: When you apply for an apartment, landlords often charge an application fee.

This fee covers the cost of processing your application and running a credit check. It can range from $30 to $50.

6. Moving Costs: Don't forget to budget for the cost of moving. Whether you hire movers or rent a truck and do it yourself, moving isn't free. The costs can vary widely depending on how far you're moving and how much stuff you have.

Signing a Lease

Signing a lease is a significant commitment. A lease is a legally binding contract that outlines the terms under which you can use the apartment. It includes the duration of your stay, the amount of rent, rules about pets, subletting policies, and other important stipulations.

- Read the lease Carefully: Before signing, read through the lease thoroughly. Look for any clauses that could affect you, such as restrictions on guests, rules about noise, and penalties for breaking the lease early.
- Understand the Terms: Make sure you understand all the terms and conditions of the lease. If there's something you don't understand, don't hesitate to ask the landlord or consult a knowledgeable adult or a lawyer.
- Document Apartment Condition: When you move in, document the condition of the apartment carefully. Take photos and make notes of any existing damages to ensure you are not held responsible for them later. This can help you get your full security deposit back when you move out.

Renting your first apartment involves careful financial planning and understanding the responsibilities of tenancy. By preparing ahead and understanding all associated costs and lease terms, you can make your first renting experience a positive and successful step towards independence.

Being Responsible

Once you're in your own apartment, you need to take responsibility for the expenses. Ensuring that you consistently pay your rent on time is essential not only for maintaining a good relationship with your landlord but also because landlords rely on this income to manage their own bills. Timely rent payments build trust and increase the likelihood that your landlord will want to renew your lease when the time comes.

If you pay your rent late, be aware that your landlord may impose additional fees or penalties, as typically outlined in your rental agreement. To avoid this:

Set a Reminder: Organize reminders for yourself a few days before the rent is due and another on the due date to ensure payment has been made.

Use Automatic Payments: Setting up an automatic bank transfer for rent payments can be a reliable way to ensure you always pay on time. As long as you have sufficient funds in your account, your rent will be paid without you having to remember each month.

Getting Your Deposit Back

When you move out, you should receive your security deposit back, provided there are no damages beyond normal wear and tear. To ensure you recover your full deposit:

- Understand the Deposit Terms: Your rental agreement outlines the conditions under which your deposit may be withheld. If anything is unclear, ask your landlord for clarification.
- Document Existing Damage: Upon moving in, immediately document any existing damages and report them to your landlord. Keep a copy of this report to use as a reference when you move out.
- Repair Damages: Address any damages you've caused, if possible and permitted.
- Give Proper Notice: Make sure you provide adequate notice before moving out, as specified in your lease. This courtesy helps your landlord prepare to find a new tenant and avoids any penalties for you.
- Clean Thoroughly: Before leaving, clean the apartment thoroughly. If the landlord deems the apartment not clean enough, he may deduct cleaning costs from your deposit.
- Conduct a Walk-Through: Request a final walk-through with your landlord using the initial damage report as a reference. This step helps ensure any deductions from your deposit are fair and agreed upon.

Managing these responsibilities effectively ensures a positive rental experience and a good relationship with your landlord, setting a solid foundation for your future rentals.

FinLit Fast Track

1. Your First Car – Download and fill out the car buying worksheet from https://FinLitFastTrack.com/buy-a-car. It will help you determine how much money you need up front and what your ongoing expenses will be.

2. Your First Apartment – The apartment worksheet will help you do the same thing for your new place. Get it here: https://FinLitFastTrack.com/apartment. If you need help estimating utilities, check out the interactive map through this link: https://FinLitFastTrack.com/utilities.

3. College ROI – If you're on the fence about going to college, check out this database: https://FinLitFastTrack.com/college-roi. It contains earnings and return on investment (ROI) information on over 40,000 degree programs.

In this chapter, you delved into the world of big purchases, gaining the knowledge and tools to make informed decisions about significant financial investments such as buying a car and renting an apartment.

In Part VI, we explore how you can prepare for the future through retirement planning and giving back. You'll explore the importance of preparing for your financial future, understand retirement accounts, and develop strategies to secure your retirement.

PART SIX

CHAPTER 12
START EARLY, RETIRE RICH

" *Retirement is wonderful if you have two essentials—much to live on and much to live for.*

UNKNOWN

Starting to save for retirement might seem premature when it's potentially 45+ years away. Still, there's a massive advantage to beginning early: compound interest. The magic of compound interest over such a long span can significantly increase your savings.

When you're young, you likely have fewer expenses compared to adults. This can be a golden opportunity to save more. Even if it's just a small amount, starting now makes a difference. Over time, with the power of compound interest, even modest savings can grow into a substantial fund.

Imagine being in a position to retire comfortably at 55 or younger. You could choose to retire early or continue working for a few more years to maximize your savings. Many people nearing retirement express concerns about not having enough money to sustain their desired lifestyle, often leading them to postpone retirement. By saving from a young age, you can look forward to a comfortable retirement, free from financial stress.

Early retirement may sound like a dream, but it's within reach if you start saving now. This early financial discipline could make your transition to retirement much smoother and more secure, offering you a sense of peace and security in your later years.

Calculating how much you need for retirement can be complex, but there are a couple of helpful guidelines to start with. One common approach is to live on about 80% of your current annual income during retirement. So, if you're earning $200,000 a year before you retire, you would aim to have about $160,000 each year in retirement.

As your income grows, it's a good idea to adjust your retirement savings goal accordingly. To figure out how much total savings you'll need, you can use the 4% rule, which is a popular method for safe withdrawal rates. According to this rule, you should save enough so that withdrawing 4% of your total retirement fund each year covers your annual expenses. For example, to have $160,000 annually, you would need about $4 million saved, assuming you rely solely on this fund and expect a 5% return on your investments.

However, relying solely on interest or returns from a large retirement fund is not the only approach to funding your retirement. Another effective strategy is generating passive income, which we explored in Chapter 8. This includes options like rental properties and dividend-paying stocks. Additionally, you can earn revenue from businesses you own but do not manage daily or from royalties. These diverse sources of passive income can significantly bolster your retirement funding strategy, giving you more control over your financial future.

Generating passive income for retirement has some great benefits, and here's why it's a smart move:

- Less Pressure on Savings: Having passive income means you don't have to rely as much on your saved money, which can help your retirement fund last longer and give you more financial security.
- Keeps Up with Rising Costs: Some passive income, like money from rental properties, tends to increase as prices go up over the years. This helps make sure you have enough money to cover things as they become more expensive.
- Steady Money Flow: With passive income, you get a more consistent flow of money. If one source dips, you might have others that are still bringing in cash, keeping things stable.
- Tax Breaks: Investing in things like real estate can offer tax benefits, such as deductions that could lower how much tax you owe.
- Better Lifestyle: Extra income sources mean you can spend more on fun stuff during retirement, like traveling or hobbies, without worrying about draining your primary savings.
- Pass It On: Dividend-paying assets like properties or stocks can be left to your family, continuing to benefit them even after you're gone.
- Protection Against Market Changes: If the stock market

gets rocky or the economy dips, having different income sources means you still have a steady income.

- Keeps You Engaged: Managing passive income sources like a rental property or a small business can keep you active and engaged, which can be rewarding and fun during retirement.

By diversifying your retirement income through savings and passive income sources, you can create a more resilient financial foundation for your later years. This approach not only helps manage the risk of outliving your savings but can also provide a more comfortable and potentially luxurious retirement lifestyle.

RETIREMENT ACCOUNTS

There are a few ways in which you can start saving for retirement. The first is to open your own savings account and start saving early. Another practical approach is to take advantage of retirement accounts like 401(k)s and IRAs, which not only help you save but also offer tax benefits that can grow your funds over time. These accounts are designed specifically for retirement and are a popular choice because they can significantly increase the amount you save due to their tax advantages.

401(k)

When you start working full-time, one of the benefits your employer might offer is a 401(k) retirement plan. Deciding whether to open a 401(k) depends on your financial goals. Still, it's an option worth considering, especially if your employer offers a contribution match. When an employer matches your contributions, it's like getting free money. For every dollar you put into your 401(k), your employer adds a certain amount, often doubling your contribution up to a specific percentage of your salary.

The contributions to your 401(k) are made with pre-tax dollars directly from your salary. This setup is convenient because the money is transferred automatically before you even see it in your paycheck, which simplifies the saving process. Moreover, because these contributions are pre-tax, they reduce your total taxable income. This means you pay less income tax now while your money grows tax-deferred until you withdraw it in retirement.

Additionally, a 401(k) is beneficial because it offers tax advantages and often includes a selection of investment options tailored to different risk tolerances and retirement timelines. This makes it a powerful tool for steadily building your retirement savings. By participating in a 401(k), especially with an employer match, you effectively accelerate your savings goals, making it a smart financial strategy for long-term growth.

IRAs

Individual Retirement Accounts (IRAs) are special savings accounts to help you plan for retirement with some tax perks. There are two main types of IRAs: Traditional IRAs and Roth IRAs. Here's a look at each type and what makes them different:

Traditional IRA: When you put money into a Traditional IRA, you might get a tax break right away. This means you can deduct the amount you contribute from your income, so you pay less in taxes this year. The money in your IRA grows without being taxed until you take it out when you retire. For 2023, you can put in up to $6,500. This type of IRA is suitable if you think you'll be in a lower tax bracket when you retire than you are now because you'll pay taxes on the money when you withdraw it at that lower rate.

Roth IRA: With Roth IRAs, you contribute money that has already been taxed. When you withdraw the money in retirement, you won't owe any taxes on it. Additionally, there are no taxes on the growth of the money in the account. Like the Traditional IRA, the limit for contributions in 2023 is $6,500. Roth IRAs are great if you expect to be in a higher tax bracket when you retire because you avoid paying higher taxes later.

Who qualifies to have an IRA? Almost anyone with earned income (from a job or self-employment) can open an IRA. If you're a teen with a part-time job, you can start one, too. For Roth IRAs, there are income limits — if you make too much, you can't contribute. In 2023, if you're single, you need to make less than $153,000 to contribute the total amount and less than $218,000 to contribute a reduced amount.

Self-Directed IRA: A self-directed IRA lets you invest in a broader range of things, not just stocks and bonds. You can invest in real estate, precious metals, and more. This IRA needs you to make all the investment decisions and follow strict rules to avoid penalties. Both Traditional and Roth IRAs can be self-directed. It's a good fit if you really understand investing and want more control over your retirement savings.

Opening an IRA is a straightforward process that can set you up for a secure future. First, you'll need to choose where to open your IRA, which could be with a bank, a brokerage firm, or a financial services company that offers IRA accounts. Once you've chosen a provider, you can usually start the process online, by phone, or in person. You'll need to provide some personal information, including your Social Security number, and decide whether you want a Traditional or Roth IRA based on your current income and future financial goals.

Next, you'll set up how you want to fund your account—this could be through a transfer from another account, a check, or a direct deposit from your earnings. After your account is open, you can choose your investments. Many providers offer resources to help you decide or professional management if you're unsure about doing it yourself. Opening an IRA early, even with small amounts, is an excellent step towards building your retirement savings.

Keogh Plans and SEP IRAs

Keogh plans (or HR-10 plans) are retirement accounts for self-employed individuals or business owners. They allow for higher contribution limits than IRAs, making them attractive for those who can afford to save more.

Another similar account is the Simplified Employee Pension (SEP) IRA, typically used by small business owners and self-employed individuals. It's easier to set up and maintain than a Keogh plan. It still offers substantial tax benefits and higher contribution limits than traditional IRAs.

While these accounts might not be relevant for you as a teen, they're part of the broader picture of retirement planning. Knowing about them can be beneficial as you start to navigate your career path, especially if you decide to go into business for yourself or pursue freelancing. They're here for informational purposes only, so you're aware of the options available as you plan for financial success in the future.

FinLit Fast Track

Activities

1. Get an idea of how much you need to save for retirement with this calculator: https://FinLitFastTrack.com/retirement-calc. What did you learn from this exercise?

2. Open an IRA account. Decide what your first retirement investment will be and research the different companies that offer an IRA for it. Since this decision can be hard to undo if you choose the wrong one, it's best to ask your parents for help on this one.

3. Just like we did for your savings account in chapter 7, set an investment goal. It may be an amount you'd like to have set aside by a certain date or even just a deadline for opening an account. Don't put the date too far in the future, but still give yourself time to achieve your goal. Make sure you write it down and post it where you can see it regularly. The format should be like this:

*On or before (date), I will*_____

Questions

1. Which retirement strategy is more appealing to you right now – building a large retirement fund, buying assets that generate passive income, or a combination of both?

2. Looking back on the section about inflation, how do you think it could affect your retirement goals?

3. If you had to guess, do you think your expenses will go up or down when you retire? Ask some retired people you know about their experience.

You learned about the importance of preparing for retirement, understanding retirement accounts, and developing a plan to achieve your retirement goals.

The next chapter explores the aspect of giving back. Giving back is not only a way to make a positive impact but also an essential aspect of a well-rounded and fulfilling financial life. Let's embark on this enlightening journey into the world of giving back and the power of making a difference.

CHAPTER 13
MAKING A DIFFERENCE THROUGH GIVING

It's easier to take than to give. It's nobler to give than to take. The thrill of taking lasts a day. The thrill of giving lasts a lifetime.

JOAN MARQUES, DEAN OF WOODBURY UNIVERSITY'S SCHOOL OF BUSINESS

Donating to charity isn't just about helping others—it's also about participating in a broader community and impacting the world positively. When you donate, you're not just giving money; you're supporting causes and helping improve lives. For instance, your donation could go towards medical research, support education in underprivileged areas, or provide disaster relief.

THE BENEFITS OF DONATING

The philosophy of "givers gain" suggests that when you give, you receive more in return. This doesn't always mean financial returns; it often refers to personal growth, happiness, and satisfaction. Donating to charity can bring immense joy, making you feel more connected to your community and giving you a profound sense of purpose. Studies have shown that giving can boost your mood, make you feel more socially connected, and even benefit your physical health.

Donating to charity can also be a powerful way of leaving a legacy. This doesn't just apply to adults with a lifetime of savings —it can start at any age. By regularly supporting a cause you care about, you create a pattern that can define part of your life's work. This could be something you're known for, like supporting animal welfare, promoting education, or funding clean water projects, giving your life a profound sense of significance and purpose.

Sharing your charitable activities with your family can be a powerful bonding experience. By discussing the causes you care about and deciding together where to donate, you're not just helping others, but also bringing your family closer. It's a way to pass down values of empathy and social responsibility, and to teach younger members the importance of generosity.

OPTIONS FOR PASSING ALONG WEALTH

As you grow older and perhaps move into careers that allow you to accumulate wealth, you'll find there are structured ways to manage how you pass on your wealth—not only to your family but also to charitable causes. Some options include:

- Donor-Advised Funds (DAFs): These are private funds administered by a third party that manages donations on your behalf. You can contribute to the fund as often as you like and recommend grants to various charities over time.
- Trusts: You can set up a charitable trust that provides you with tax benefits while also supporting your chosen causes. There are several types of trusts, each with specific advantages and purposes.
- Foundations: If you find yourself in a position to make substantial charitable contributions, starting a foundation is a way to manage large donations. Foundations can be family-run, allowing you to involve multiple generations in philanthropy.

TEACHING THE NEXT GENERATION

It's also crucial to empower others about the benefits of donating. Whether it's speaking at school, writing a blog, or starting a club dedicated to charitable work, spreading the word increases the impact you can have. Educating your peers creates a ripple effect, encouraging a new generation of givers and instilling a sense of responsibility and empowerment in them.

FinLit Fast Track

Activities

1. Become a philanthropist today. Revisit your budget and carve out at least a small portion for charity. You can donate a little each month or save up and make a bigger impact a couple times a year.

2. If you would like to make a big impact now, but only have a small amount of money, organize a fund raiser to support your cause. Https://FinLitFastTrack.com/fundraisers has a list of ideas to spark your creativity.

3. "Givers Gain" is a real phenomenon, although most people don't believe in it. The reason is there is often a delay between your act of giving and your reward. Start noticing what comes back to you after you give to others. Remember to thank the Universe when it does!

Questions

1. What causes or organizations are important to you?
2. Can you think of easy ways to pass on what you learned in this book to younger siblings or friends?
3. Beside donating money, what other ways can you think of to help your favorite organizations?

Donating to charity and engaging in philanthropy are powerful ways to make a difference, not just in the lives of others, but also in your own. Starting as a teen, you can grow into these practices, enhancing your understanding of the world and developing a life-long habit of generosity. Whether it's through small regular donations, setting up a fund, or eventually creating a foundation, every step you take builds towards a legacy of giving. Remember, every contribution counts, and the habits you form now will shape the type of adult you become.

CONCLUSION

 Go confidently in the direction of your dreams! Live the life you've imagined.

HENRY DAVID THOREAU, AMERICAN PHILOSOPHER

By now, you should have a solid understanding of finances and feel a sense of accomplishment in your journey towards financial literacy. Remember, it's perfectly fine to revisit chapters if you want to refresh your memory on specific topics. It's also crucial to keep learning—this book is just the beginning of your financial education journey. Being financially savvy is a lifelong pursuit that can only enhance your success.

Approach money with a positive mindset. Your mindset determines your success. Viewing money negatively will make it hard to see the good that money can do. Money itself isn't evil; it's simply a tool for managing our lives. As you start earning, you'll see why it's essential to manage it wisely rather than letting it control you. Whether you're earning from a job or running your own business, understanding how to manage your finances from a young age is critical. Remember, this knowledge can pave the way for your financial freedom.

Whether you're an employee or a freelancer, it's important to understand that deductions like taxes and benefits will affect your take-home pay. Filing a tax return every year, even if you're unsure if you need to, is a responsible financial practice. It's a good idea to seek professional advice or ask a parent to guide you through the process initially. This way, you can gain the necessary knowledge to manage your taxes independently in the future.

Learning how to manage a bank account, whether it's checking or savings, is fundamental. Creating a budget will help you track your spending and save effectively. A budget helps you track where your money goes, making it easier to set financial goals and allocate funds for things like savings. Keep in mind, the goal isn't just to save significant amounts but to develop the habit of saving. Your adult self will thank you for knowing how to build up an emergency fund and how to save for specific purchases.

Investing is a powerful way to grow your money and secure your financial future. However, it does come with risks, so it's essential to educate yourself and make informed choices. A well-rounded investment portfolio includes a mix of different types of investments—both stocks (paper assets) and tangible assets like real estate. Diversifying helps balance risk and can provide steady income or potential growth over time.

If you invest in tangible assets, it's wise to insure them. Whether through specific insurance policies or part of your renters' insurance, this protects you financially in case of damage or loss.

Your credit score is crucial as it reflects your reliability with money and affects things like loan interest rates and insurance premiums. Maintain a good credit score by managing debt wisely, paying bills on time, and spending responsibly.

Starting early on financial responsibilities, including saving for retirement, sets a strong foundation. By taking these steps now, you're demonstrating a proactive approach to your financial future.

As you finish this book, I hope you feel empowered, like you can take on your financial future with confidence. The power of financial literacy is within your reach, and with every choice you make, you're one step closer to securing the life you've always dreamed of. Start today and let your journey toward financial success begin!

Lastly, remember that you're never too young to start making intelligent financial decisions. Be an Emma, not a David. If you enjoyed this journey, please leave a review on Amazon to help other teens navigate their financial paths. I'm eager to hear about your progress and successes!

FAST TRACK CHECKLIST

Use this Fast Track Checklist as a flexible tool to track your progress through the book. Understand that it's absolutely okay if you can't complete every activity right now. Your learning journey is unique and as you mature and your knowledge expands, you'll have the opportunity to complete all the tasks. Remember, becoming financially literate is a process, so when you do complete everything, take a moment to celebrate your personal triumphs.

Activity	Completed
Chapter 1	
Watch the "Hidden Secrets of Money" series	
Experiment with the inflation calculator	
Chapter 2	
Determine your money personality	
Choose your personal money mantras	
Chapter 3	
Research job options	
Research business options	
Chapter 4	
Practice filling out a tax return	
List the different types of taxes	
Chapter 5	
Open a bank account	
Chapter 6	
Brainstorm ways to thwart impulse buys	
Create your budget	
Chapter 7	
Open a savings account	
Set up a cash-match pact with your parents	
Write out your savings goal	
Explore the compound interest calculator	

Chapter 8	
Create an investment category in your budget	
Research at least one investment type	
Take the risk tolerance quiz	
Buy a silver coin	
Chapter 9	
Review an insurance policy	
Inventory your belongings	
Chapter 10	
Check your credit report and score	
Determine your credit card interest rate	
Get a credit builder loan	
Chapter 11	
Research your first car	
Research your first apartment	
Explore the College ROI database	
Chapter 12	
Experiment with the retirement calculator	
Open and IRA account	
Write down your first investment goal	
Chapter 13	
Create a charity category in your budget	
Organize a fund raiser	
Notice what comes back to you when you give	

REFERENCES

Anwar, Z., Fury, E. D., & Fauziah, S. R. (2020). The fear of missing out and usage intensity of social media. *Research Gate*, *395*, 183–187. https://www.research gate.net/publication/339194370_The_Fear_of_Missing_Out_and_Usage_In tensity_of_Social_Media.

Black, M. (2024). What Is The Average Credit Card Interest Rate This Week? June 16, 2024. https://www.forbes.com/advisor/credit-cards/average-credit-card-interest-rate/.

Backman, M. (2017, July 23). *7 stats that show how today's teens are making smart money choices*. The Motley Fool. https://www.fool.com/retirement/2017/07/23/7-stats-that-show-how-todays-teens-are-making-smar.aspx.

Google Finance. (2024, June 11). Dow Jones Industrial Average Price, Real-time Quote & News - Google Finance. Www.google.com. https://www.google.com/finance/quote/.DJI:INDEXDJX?hl=en

Jacimovic, D. (2023, February 7). *25+ educational financial literacy statistics you need to learn about*. Moneytransfers.com. https://moneytransfers.com/news/2022/09/07/financial-literacy-statistics.

Maloney, M. (2015). *Guide to investing in gold & silver: Protect your financial future*. Wealth Cycles.

MyFICO. (2016). How are FICO Scores Calculated? | myFICO. Myfico.com. https://www.myfico.com/credit-education/whats-in-your-credit-score

Pay-stub.com. (n.d.). Online Pay Stub Generator. Pay-Stub.com. Retrieved June 18, 2024, from https://www.pay-stub.com/online-pay-stub-generator/

Stacey M. (2024, January 27). *Financial literacy statistics for 2023*. Self-Starters. https://self-starters.com/financial-literacy-statistics.

Yahoo Finance. (2023). Tesla, Inc. (TSLA) Stock Price, Quote, History & News. YahooFinance. https://finance.yahoo.com/quote/TSLA/

Made in the USA
Monee, IL
16 December 2024

74057154R00105